TEACHING PRIMARY MUSIC

Sara Miller McCune founded SAGE Publishing in 1965 to support the dissemination of usable knowledge and educate a global community. SAGE publishes more than 1000 journals and over 800 new books each year, spanning a wide range of subject areas. Our growing selection of library products includes archives, data, case studies and video. SAGE remains majority owned by our founder and after her lifetime will become owned by a charitable trust that secures the company's continued independence.

Los Angeles | London | New Delhi | Singapore | Washington DC | Melbourne

TEACHING PRIMARY MUSIC

ALISON DAUBNEY

Los Angeles | London | New Delhi
Singapore | Washington DC | Melbourne

Los Angeles | London | New Delhi
Singapore | Washington DC | Melbourne

SAGE Publications Ltd
1 Oliver's Yard
55 City Road
London EC1Y 1SP

SAGE Publications Inc.
2455 Teller Road
Thousand Oaks, California 91320

SAGE Publications India Pvt Ltd
B 1/I 1 Mohan Cooperative Industrial Area
Mathura Road
New Delhi 110 044

SAGE Publications Asia-Pacific Pte Ltd
3 Church Street
#10-04 Samsung Hub
Singapore 049483

Editor: James Clark
Assistant editor: Robert Patterson
Production editor: Nicola Carrier
Copyeditor: Sharon Cawood
Indexer: Silvia Benvenuto
Marketing manager: Dilhara Attygalle
Cover design: Sheila Tong
Typeset by: C&M Digitals (P) Ltd, Chennai, India
Printed by: CPI Group (UK) Ltd, Croydon, CR0 4YY

Library of Congress Control Number: 2016953508

British Library Cataloguing in Publication data

A catalogue record for this book is available from the British Library

ISBN 978-1-4739-0570-2
ISBN 978-1-4739-0571-9 (pbk)

At SAGE we take sustainability seriously. Most of our products are printed in the UK using FSC papers and boards. When we print overseas we ensure sustainable papers are used as measured by the PREPS grading system. We undertake an annual audit to monitor our sustainability.

CONTENTS

ABOUT THE AUTHOR

Alison Daubney is a qualified and experienced teacher. She has taught across all stages of education from pre-school to postgraduate. She was awarded a PhD by the University of Surrey, Roehampton, in 2008.

As an international education consultant, Alison has worked extensively for the University of Cambridge International Examinations on curriculum development, assessment reform and teacher training in Kazakhstan, Egypt and Mongolia.

Alison regularly works nationally and internationally with education, arts and cultural organisations, schools, music services and hubs, undertaking research and evaluation, developing training and leading workshops.

She is on the board of the SoundCity:Brighton and Hove Music Education Hub and a member of the DfE Education Special Advisory Group for Music Education.

Alison is involved in teacher education for pre-service and in-service teachers and has worked part time at the University of Sussex since 2008.

FOREWORD

After 20 years as a primary class teacher, I took a part-time job in the charity sector but I wanted to keep my hand in with some classroom teaching. When I asked my school if they could employ me for a day a week, I was told it would have to be for something other class teachers didn't like teaching. I was offered RE or music. I went for the RE. After all, as so many teachers pointed out, I couldn't play the piano so I wouldn't be able to manage. Fast forward five years – I still can't play the piano but I'm now teaching music. I just wish someone had given me this book. It is so great to have a book rooted in the school curriculum that is perfectly accessible for all classroom teachers whether or not they feel they have a musical background.

For years I was put off teaching music to my own class because I couldn't read music. Ally deals with this head on in the book and puts the reading of notation in its proper context. I think the way that Ally compares literacy and musical literacy is really helpful and will make a lot of sense to non-specialist classroom teachers and musical specialist teachers alike.

I first met Ally at a training session she was giving for the Incorporated Society of Musicians (ISM) on the new national curriculum for music. I am still using her practical and innovative ideas in the classroom: 'The answer is in the room!' 'What do you need and what can you offer?' are fantastically useful approaches that take us forward.

Ally helpfully starts the book by reminding us that we will never encounter a musically empty child. Too many music schemes give the impression that children have no experience of music other than in the music classroom, forgetting that most of us live sound-enriched lives. By starting her book with this chapter, looking at the place music has in our lives, we can start to create a music curriculum in our schools that doesn't see the child as an empty vessel.

Chapter 3 on singing and vocal development will really put you at your ease. I found it excruciatingly uncomfortable to sing in front of adults when I first started and would often find 'reasons' for support staff to leave the room. This chapter contains excellent advice and lots of helpful tips.

The chapter I found the most helpful is Chapter 5. This really got to the heart of my greatest anxieties about teaching music. I found the idea of composing quite terrifying. Ally demystifies it and puts it in its correct perspective. Even the way she describes improvising as doodling or fooling around with sound helps us put it into context. Ally is spot on when she reminds us that it is worth thinking about how we teach primary school pupils to write.

Ally reminds us in Chapter 8 that assessment is not a dirty word. I can't believe I am alone in coming to dread the word and the mind-numbing tasks associated with it. By starting from the premise that the word 'assessment' has been hijacked, Ally goes on to show us, using practical examples, how we can use assessment to help us teach more effectively. I had not come across Swanwick's mantra – 'to teach is to assess' – before; I am considering printing it out as a banner and displaying it in my school entrance.

I can see shares in polar graph paper going through the roof. Ally has come up with a simple, innovative way to create meaningful assessment that children can be fully involved with. Using a 'theory of personal construct' is an incredibly exciting way to start mapping out progression, with the children taking responsibility for their own development: way more exciting and useful than any tick chart.

This book is designed for the non-specialist music teacher who doesn't consider themselves to be a musician. The anecdotes and scenarios provide stimulating jumping-off points. I think it will also be valuable to music tutors who provide whole-class ensemble teaching (WCET). It also has plenty to say to those who are responsible for planning music provision in school, particularly music coordinators who have the task of trying to help other teachers have the confidence to teach music.

Whilst there will always be a place for piano-playing musical specialists in our schools, it is more important that we have armies of class teachers ready, willing and able to start exploring sound. I look forward to this book being widely read by head teachers, school governors, experienced teachers, newly qualified teachers and music coordinators. Every single society throughout time immemorial has made music. It's about time we got our act together and worked out how we are going to give all our primary school children the opportunity to make music at school. This book will help enormously.

Jackie Schneider (primary school teacher)

ACKNOWLEDGEMENTS

Music was always playing in our house; I am almost word perfect on Queen's back catalogues, courtesy of my older brother Jeff's penchant for loud music blaring from his bedroom every waking hour. I am deeply grateful to my family for their unwavering support throughout my life, and particularly to my parents – my mum, Ann, and my late father, Bill. I am sure that *Roses from the South* will stay with me forever; it was the piece Dad could always find his way to on the piano even with no sight.

Inspiring teachers are crucial and I was lucky to find many along the way. Music oozed from the pores of Manor Field Primary School where Mr Barker, Miss Harrison, Mr Doughty and Mrs Bell developed my love of music. Revisiting my own education has cemented my views about the fundamental importance of rich and creative experiences for all children from an early age. At secondary school, I was lucky enough to be taught by Roland Bryce. I have immense gratitude for his encouragement and guidance throughout my musical journey. He was then, and continues to be, a truly inspiring musician and teacher.

I also want to thank a few other people. I am indebted to Professor Martin Fautley for his encouragement in helping me to 'find my voice' in the world of music education and for giving me the confidence to write this book in my own way. I also want to thank my colleague Duncan Mackrill at the University of Sussex for constantly giving me new things to think about and supporting everything I do. It is always appreciated. I am very grateful to Jackie Schneider for reading the chapters as they emerged, from her perspective as a teacher. For sure, Rob Patterson at Sage has the patience of a saint and I want to thank him too!

Emma and Lindsey, no matter where you are in the world, I appreciate your wonderful friendship and the music we have made and shared.

This book is dedicated to my amazing husband, Greg. It is no understatement to say that life has thrown us a few curveballs over the past few years and I know that I am lucky to still be here and even luckier to explore the world with you.

1
MUSIC: ITS PLACE IN OUR LIVES AND EDUCATION

Peering through the school hall door, I noticed the beaming smiles of Mrs Clark's Year 3 class stomping around the room to 'Nellie the Elephant', which was blaring from the speakers. Most were marching in time with the music and each other. Weaving in between their haphazard pattern was Mrs Clark, joining in with evident delight, making eye contact with children as she marched around, pumping her arms in time and with gusto. With the music in full flow, the room suddenly fell silent. Abruptly, the activity stopped and the children and teacher froze mid-move.

Introduction

What did you see and hear in your mind as you read this? Did it portray your pre-conceived image of a music lesson; one filled with sound, energy, movement and enjoyment? Were you the teacher in the middle of the room, joining in, communicating, modelling – integral to this musical community?

Or perhaps it was accompanied by a sigh as you lamented on the thought of teaching music (which, for some, is a probable reason for opening a book such as this)?

This book is a journey into our sound world. It is about musical journeys, in the broadest sense. My belief is that what you bring to, and take from, this musical journey is of fundamental significance and importance to you and to the children you work with. Children need adult role models who are not all 'professional musicians'. They need you, their primary school teacher, to be a part of the musical community in their school and classroom, taking part, leading learning and learning from and with the children.

Perhaps you hope that this book will give you ideas and the confidence to work with your class. I hope it will, but my ambition is that, by the end of it, you will also believe in your power to positively enhance education, learning and life. Music changes lives. As a teacher, you have the power to sprinkle magic through offering a musical education.

Remember though that if you don't teach music, you cannot guarantee that someone else will, and by not teaching music many children will have seriously impoverished experiences. Their lives march on. They will never be 7 years old again. The time and opportunity for lasting and sustained positive impact is right here, right now (as Fat Boy Slim famously stated). You may not feel particularly confident about teaching music, but I urge you to try. An enthusiastic teacher and a 'have a go' attitude will get you a long way and will significantly benefit the children you work with.

I hope that along the way you find what you came looking for in this book: most of all, inherent self-belief in yourself as a musical being and the desire and confidence to nurture and share musical experiences.

Objectives

Through this chapter you will:

- consider the importance of music education
- examine and challenge commonly held assumptions about music
- explore what musical learning is and could be
- understand how music is integral to our fast-changing world
- gain confidence that you already know a great deal.

Why music?

We are in a world where educational powerhouses appear to encourage society to value academic prowess over all else, a world where children are frequently tested against a set of standardised, age-related norms in a very narrow set of 'high stakes' subjects (Kneyber, 2016). It is easy to forget that music is something very special and ever-present. Music is always with us – throughout and between every rite of passage from before we are born until after we die.

Following the 1988 Education Reform Act, music has been constantly present as a statutory subject in schools, falling within the National Curriculum, and was present in some form or another in many schools before the National Curriculum came into being. Nevertheless, we need to question its impact and position. Does music's position in the curriculum cement its importance? Why do we teach music in schools? Why is it that many independent schools, with autonomy over teaching and learning, highly value music education and commit valuable curriculum and co-curricular time to it? Conversely, we hear weekly horror stories of state schools being under inordinate pressure to focus on the core subjects at the expense of the arts, creativity and culture, providing a narrow, constricted and frankly often dull and uninspiring education.

Notwithstanding the importance of music for its own sake, there is also a plethora of research demonstrating how music contributes to our personal, psychological, social, educational and emotional development and wellbeing (Fiske, 1999; Hallam, 2015). This is just the kind of thing we think head teachers want to hear, but it is not in itself a justification for teaching and learning music. Where do you stand on the 'music is good for your development so it should be in education' debate? Parents of young children probably don't sing them songs at bathtime so that they will be better at mathematics. Clearly, then, music's place in the curriculum is not there primarily because of its transferable learning possibilities.

Sometimes people consider that music is a special gift and you are either musical or you're not. Some people consider that music can only be taught by 'special people' with a high degree of musical training and prowess. These are both nonsense. Frankly, we don't do ourselves many favours here. In primary schools, we sometimes wheel in 'specialists' to teach music, leaving everyone else to think that they can't do it or don't need to (Hennessy, 2000). We perpetuate ridiculous ideas that we aren't musical if we can't read music, or that the teacher who can play the piano in assembly is the only one who can be labelled as a 'musician' in school. Yet musical experiences and the level of music education of generalist student teachers is often rich and diverse (Henley, 2016), and Ofsted (2009, 2012) notes that the quality of music teaching is often better in primary schools than secondary schools, where music is almost always taught by teachers with a high level of music qualification and subject-specific training.

It is of course the case that a minority of people seem extremely gifted at music and we could all name a few of these who appear on the world stage as virtuoso performers, conductors or composers. But music is for everyone. It can be accessed, enjoyed, learnt and taught by all. We need to put all 'labels' and preconceptions aside and recognise that music is a part of us all. To think otherwise is detrimental, as Howe, Davidson and Sloboda (1998: 407) report from a study entitled 'Innate talents – reality or myth?'

> The evidence we have surveyed in this target article does not support the talent account, according to which excelling is a consequence of possessing innate gifts … categorising some children as innately talented is discriminatory … Such categorisation is unfair and wasteful, preventing young people from pursuing a goal because of teachers' or parents' unjustified conviction that they would not benefit from the superior opportunities given to those who are deemed to be talented.

Regardless of whether or not it is formally taught, music is a constant presence in our lives (DeNora, 2000). Have you ever watched a 4-year-old spontaneously spinning around and singing along to their favourite Disney track, making sense of it within their own limited language? Babies babbling and smiling as their parents sing or beatbox to them? Teenagers absorbed in the music broadcasting through their headphones on a quiet train, occasionally slipping into the accidental verbalising of the lyrics they are listening to? Children already love music – our job in school (and life) is to nurture and help develop this love. It is no easy task though – music is highly personal, offering endless possibilities and tangents.

The flip side, though, is the fragility and responsibility that comes with this. I am arguing that *you* are the important person, the one who should nurture children's interests, skills, confidence and creativity and develop ownership of their music. Yet there is a tension here too. It is *their* music, *their* soundtrack, not yours. You have your own, which is also constantly evolving as you negotiate your way through life. There are times to scaffold learning, to collaborate or stand back and times to learn from others, times to listen, suggest, sympathise and offer support and guidance, to set up creative landscapes, to share skills and knowledge or signpost others who can. Clearly, music education is multi-layered and complex but your contribution, enthusiasm and guidance are both integral and fundamentally important.

The importance of positive experiences in music education

Reflecting on musical experiences often reveals how important these were in shaping people's attitudes to teaching music and themselves in relation to music (I am hesitant to say 'as a musician' because I think the term itself is value-laden and unhelpful). Mostly, in my experience of working with teachers and trainee teachers, people fall into four distinct groups:

1. People with limited memories of music education as a pupil, where it appears to have been vacuous both within and beyond school at that point in their lives.
2. People with positive memories relating to at least one significant part of their own education (either primary school, secondary school or both). This often relates to playing musical instruments, singing or performing; they may recall fondly either an influential person or group of people – often a teacher, family or friends – and the social aspect of music is also evident.
3. People who had positive musical learning experiences or influences outside of school but failed to see the relevance of music in school; it seems that their musical identity memorably evolved *in spite of* their music education in school.
4. Unfortunately, though, many people fall into the fourth group; education research shows over and over again that: 'people who at a young age were told that they were not musical seldom enjoy a childhood of growing musicianship' (Lehmann, Sloboda and Woody, 2007: 49).

It is sad that many people recall impoverished experiences of music education themselves or were left with the impression that they are not musical. Unsurprisingly, this blights their own self-view in relation to their abilities and confidence to teach music. Pitts (2012) reveals the powerful potential of music education to shape identities – and not always positively.

Lehmann, Sloboda and Woody's hard-hitting statement must be at the forefront of our minds when teaching or interacting with people, regardless of the subject. As teachers, we are extremely powerful when it comes to how we make people feel. What we say and how we act can be misconstrued, misunderstood and taken to heart. A child only needs to hear once that they are 'tone-deaf', cannot play in tune, have no sense of rhythm, should mime instead of sing, or be refused entry to the choir because it will spoil the sound, and they will potentially carry that crushing judgement with them throughout their lives. Music needs to be accessible, engaging, challenging, inclusive and, perhaps most importantly, overwhelmingly positive for all. Otherwise, it may inadvertently send negative messages and contribute to adults spending many years avoiding situations in which they feel musically and socially vulnerable or embarrassed.

TASK 1.1

Reflect on your own musical experiences:

1. What can you remember about music education/musical influences when you were of primary school age?

- • How did you feel about yourself in relation to music at that time? Were you influenced (positively or negatively) by anyone or anything in school? How did you engage with music at this age?

- • What about music at home and out of school? Who and what influenced you? What kinds of memories of music do you have from out of school?

- • What three words or phrases would you use to sum up your feelings about music at this age?

2. Think through the same questions above in relation to yourself as a secondary school pupil.

3. Then move on to consider: At what point in your educational career did you stop studying or participating in music in school? Or did you continue? What about out of school? What influenced these decisions? How did you feel about them at the time? What about now?

4. Thinking about all of these experiences, what do they tell you about your own music education and the impact of people and events to shape your musical identities and feelings across time?

Building on what children already know

> ... a music teacher never meets musically ignorant, untutored or uneducated pupils: on the contrary, when pupils come to school they all possess a rich and in some ways sophisticated musical knowledge, acquired from a variety of outside-school musical activities (Folkestad, 2006: 136)

It could be rephrased as 'a pupil never meets a musically ignorant, untutored or uneducated teacher', but unless we share our musical identities with children, they probably assume that teachers don't listen to popular music!

Children and teachers come to school with a wide range of musical experiences – all different – and gathered as they live their everyday lives. Children are not 'empty musical vessels' when they start school or indeed at any point in their school career; they have years of experience as consumers of, and partakers in, music. There is always something for us to build on, and helping children to build connections between different parts of their 'musical' lives is a very important part of music education; it is fascinating to explore the influences and habits of families and friends as children start school through listening carefully to the eclectic examples they sing, hum, adapt and talk about.

It's a mistake to think that we have to 'teach' young people everything they need to know about music. We also need to be careful that we don't abuse our power by denying them opportunities and access to knowledge, falling into the trap of thinking that only certain 'types' of music, experiences and skills are suitable for certain children. Instead, we should consider the opportunities for 'co-constructing' rather than 'delivering' musical learning. Offering all children frequent opportunities to engage in music is crucial; to a great extent, musical development is linked to experience, and this is particularly noticeable in pre-school children.

The value, purpose and importance of music in schools

In order to properly consider the value, purpose and importance of music in schools, we need to ponder the wider philosophical underpinning on which our thoughts about education and learning are predicated. This is not about seeking the one 'right' answer, but about examining our own thoughts about education and exploring and defining our own values.

TASK 1.2

You may wish to do this activity with others and collate your key ideas.
Think about the following:

1. What do you value in education? Mind map these ideas.

2. Are there any additional things you value in a music education? Add these.

3. Display these to remind you throughout the year and reflect on the extent to which your values are borne out in your teaching.

Here are some frequently mentioned points:

- inclusive; accessible and challenging for all children
- enjoyment
- creative/promoting creativity/inquisitiveness
- engaging/worthwhile
- practical – learning through doing
- exploring 'feelings' and 'self' through music.

TASK 1.3

Think about and write down your ideas about:

- the *purpose* of music education in primary schools

- what a music education in school should include and be based on

- how music education in school could relate to music in our 'real lives'.

What is the purpose of music education in school – is it there to provide children with the experiences of playing musical instruments? To sing together? To create their own music? To be part of something amazing with other pupils? To experience different music to what they might find for themselves? To perpetuate or build on what they already know? To make sure children get a dose of high art and culture? And how do we get past 'edutainment' and make sure that musical learning is underpinned by established and worthwhile pedagogical principles and learning experiences? Musical learning has many purposes, but one thing is for sure – *school is the place where all children must have access to music education*, otherwise it becomes an elitist pastime where only children of families that can afford to pay will have access to it.

Importance is a strange thing. What is important, and who is it important to? There are various answers to these questions and they link, in part, to values: your values, the school's values, the children's values, the parents' values. Unfortunately, though, these sometimes get usurped when higher perceived orders of 'importance' enter the fray. Too often, these are linked to external assessment and judgements, particularly Ofsted inspections and whole-school judgements, including statutory government-enforced tests for children at different ages and the significant impact of these on how the school is viewed and ranked externally.

In the Ofsted report *Good Teaching in Art, Dance, Drama and Music*, Clay et al. (1998: 3) signal strong support for the arts, noting that:

> The arts ... are intrinsic components of human culture, heritage and creativity. They mirror the whole repertoire of human experience, and are worthy of study in their own right. It is difficult to imagine the world without arts.

This reminds me of Richard Stilgoe's (no date) *Sonnet on a World Without Music* – well worth a read.

Does your school exemplify the importance of the arts and embody this statement through what happens in and out of the classroom? Do the parents place any importance on the arts? And, most importantly, what about the children themselves? If you gave a class of children free rein to design a day in school, in all likelihood it would be a day filled with joy and collaboration, with music and art holding centre-stage. Another challenge therefore is to capitalise on music and the arts to hook children into learning.

If the arts in school are to mirror real life, we need to be mindful of the diversity of music itself, and of musical practices and experiences. Our musical development transcends paths influenced by our own journeys through the world; children (and teachers) bring a rich and diverse range of skills, knowledge and experiences into the classroom, based on their own 'complex auditory ecosystem' (Campbell, 2010: 77). Marsh (2010: 43) notes the following influences on children's musical games:

> parents, siblings, and other relatives; mediated sources found on television, CDs, cassettes, films, DVDs, videos, the radio, and Internet; peers in the playground and classroom; teachers, and the materials which form part of school curricula; and experiences which may be gained in countries of birth, on visits to countries of cultural origin, or on holidays in other localities.

Music in school is multi-faceted and may include music in the curriculum, through the curriculum and beyond the curriculum, for example in assemblies, clubs, performances and playground games, instrumental or vocal lessons and open-access equipment such as a music garden, an instrument corner and practice rooms. A school is, in effect, its own community with its own values. What it includes or leaves out, what it focuses on or recognises are choices made by the school community.

The National Curriculum for Music Education

Analysis of the National Curriculum for Music Education in England (DfE, 2013) as a word cloud yields the following results (Figure 1.1):

Figure 1.1   Overview of the National Curriculum for Music

Source: based on the National Curriculum for Music (DfE, 2013)

Considering the relative size of the terms, the practical nature of the subject shines through. Making and creating music are central; there is a focus on musical activities (performing, playing, singing, composing, listening, improvising) in order to develop musical understanding and fluency. We do this through using tools (instruments, voices, technologies). Other terminology relates to outcomes, i.e. *how* we should be doing something (e.g. with expression, control, accuracy, fluency). It is clear, then, that through *doing* music we also develop our knowledge and understanding *of* music. Yet, the quest for tangible knowledge, understanding and skills should not get in the way of recognising thoughts, feelings and the aesthetic dimensions of engagement – all of which are important and worthy aspects of a music education and explored further in Chapter 2.

'Critical engagement' is a central aspiration throughout musical learning. It is the essence of what we do when thinking and acting musically. This is supported by, and supports, many other aspirations, including: creativity, engaging with live and recorded music, developing aural memory, developing an awareness of social, historical and cultural aspects of music and being able to communicate in and through music, using staff and 'other' musical notations to support this when appropriate. This viewpoint is explored in detail in Chapter 6, aimed at busting the myth 'I can't read music so I can't teach it'.

Music is contextualised by its historical, social and cultural roots. The phrases 'the great composers' and 'the best in the musical canon', both present in the National Curriculum (DfE, 2013), might be perceived as a nod towards Western Classical traditions, perpetuating the nonsensical idea of a 'musical hierarchy' and another reason some teachers feel ill-equipped to teach music. But what is the 'best'? And who decides? Everyone has an opinion on what should be on the musical menu and how 'good' music is. As Mills (2009: 1) states: 'I do not feel that there is a canon of music that everyone – pupils or teachers – should learn', a sentiment with which I wholeheartedly agree. A rich musical education is one that, over time, meaningfully introduces many styles, genres, idioms and traditions across times, cultures, communities and places, and which offers access to 'a range of … live and recorded music' (DfE, 2013) and the opportunities to decide for ourselves what we think of it. The important thing is that we build bridges with children between their current sound world and experiences and those with which they are not yet familiar.

'Culture' is another very value-bound word. Sometimes, music education seems to block together 'cultures and traditions', taking children on what Fautley (2011) describes as a 'Cook's Tour', with a cursory glance at different cultures and the music therein through packaging music into short, often tokenistic, units of work. These don't get to the heart of the relationships between music, time, places, cultures and people and do not help children to link up their learning. A review of 'Cultural Education in the UK' (DfE and DCMS, 2012) includes the following under the umbrella term 'cultural education': 'archaeology, architecture and the built environment, archives, craft, dance, design, digital arts, drama and theatre, film and cinemas, galleries, heritage, libraries, literature, live performance, museums, music, poetry and the visual arts' (Henley, 2012: 3).

This is a somewhat unsatisfactory and impoverished view of culture and cultural education. It misses the point that our cultural education is personal to us – it is personal and fluid, influenced by lived experiences, people, events, time and places. Such views of culture provide a blanket view that 'culture is good for children', without necessarily taking a step back to consider whose values and cultures are being imposed.

Henley's cultural education report (2012: 8) also states that:

> Schools remain the single most important place where children learn about Cultural Education. This takes the form of structured curriculum lessons in subjects such as history, English literature, art and design, design technology, drama, dance, film studies and music, alongside programmes of after school activities for children who wish to pursue a passion for a particular art form.

On-going work in Brighton and Hove aims to 'improve the lives and life-chances of children and young people in Brighton & Hove through cultural engagement and creative skills' (Our Future City, 2015a) taking a much more open approach, asking 'what are the questions we need to ask' and gathering a wider view of culture, what 'it' is to the young people and where 'it' takes place. A perhaps unsurprising eclectic view of culture is emerging – young participants consider their 'cultural education' to take place with friends, on their own and with family, with 'in school' trailing in last place (Our Future City, 2015b: 12). The report also notes that 'culture' includes activities such as playing in the park, going to Scouts and scuba diving alongside those we might expect to see such as music, crafts, arts and reading.

As Finney (2009: 31) reminds us:

> ... young people come to school, come to any educational setting, already with a culture of their own and knowing how to learn. They will have already explored a range of musical identities, reflected on these and be ready to meet new cultural experiences with critical minds.

Perhaps our focus on culture in relation to music education should heed Finney's (2009: 34) advice that:

> The challenge for the music teacher is to be resourceful and remain culturally alive, to search out new ways of being musical and to continually ask why music is made, why it is so important to those who make it and in what ways it is related to a way of life that might be similar or very different to their own or their students.

Music in a fast-changing world

Music is everywhere. The way we access and engage with music continues to significantly shift. Even recently, a book such as this would describe laptops, CDs, minidisks and the beginnings of interactive whiteboards as the new classroom revolution. Instead, the digital revolution continues to march forward; downloading and streaming music are the norm and tablets are prevalent throughout our daily lives; even pre-school children access music in this way, making choices about what they listen to, making and creating music, enculturated into a digital world from a very young age (Young, 2007).

This was unimaginable just a few years ago, when children were still in the business of saving up pocket money to go to a shop and buy a much-cherished chart track or album. The convenience of music at our fingertips changes our experiences with music. In the 1980s, my friends and I delighted in recording songs onto a cassette tape from the radio chart show on a Sunday evening and accepted that the DJ might talk over the introduction. Forwarding the tapes to the start of a song was more estimation than perfect science and the inevitable warping left the sound less than perfect, yet this was our form of 'downloading'. Vinyl records and (eventually) compact discs were the norm; through paying for a whole album, we stumbled across unfamiliar music, because the chances were that only one or two songs on the album were previously familiar. The artwork was important and influential, and music videos started to gain prominence.

Fast forward 30 years: if children want music, they don't need to buy it, nor do they have to wait until it is played again on the radio – they just search for it online and stream it. They can instantly access music and videos on mobile phones, iPods, apps, at any time and anywhere, creating playlists to share with friends without the need for a mix-tape. The internet is packed with music tutorials and information. This is another way in which they develop skills, understanding and knowledge – from mending a bicycle puncture to playing a chord on the ukulele or competing at football against strangers through their games console, this is their real world. Bringing this world into formal education is challenging, yet essential.

Communicating through the internet and mobile devices accessed anywhere is mainstream; if it is not the child themselves using social networking, the likelihood is that someone in a child's family will connect with the world from the comfort of their bean bag. There are many social networks and virtual learning environments that schools use internally and sometimes externally too, so this way of communicating is second nature to many. There is much potential to use these technologies in music education, as the following example shows:

> Animated discussion emerged from the 'Oak' table as six Year 5 children jostled for position in order to see the tablet. Millie began reading out comments from the school blog; opinions left by total strangers about the recording of Oak's 'football song' which the teacher had uploaded the previous week. As Millie read through the comments, the others half-listened and passed comment on the sentiments. Mr Tickell wandered over and asked the group to 'consider what they would do if they had ten minutes more' and an opportunity to re-record the music. As he walked away, George clicked on the recording and the group spontaneously started to sing along.

Music is a sonic art, taking place in the 'here and now' – what happens 'in the moment' has gone once the time has passed. This example demonstrates the power of technology to help capture and develop music over time and also to create authentic experiences where music is critiqued by strangers.

Music has universally existed across time and place. The 'third environment' (Hargreaves et al., 2003), the informal environment where children function musically outside of formal learning environments in and out of school, is where much musical learning and engagement take place. We should not be surprised about this since children spend a significant amount of time outside of school, and are influenced by their communities, families and friends as well as by the music they choose to engage with. This informal learning is not new; there are many musicians, famous or otherwise, who are self-taught or who have experienced significant parts of their music education through learning informally.

Music education, and education more generally, needs to consider how to capitalise on and promote informal learning within formal educational structures. We should plan and enhance opportunities for learning which are 'co-constructed *with*' pupils rather than those which are 'done *to*' pupils and, ultimately, consider what music education might be, rather than only perpetuating what we see currently.

You, the musical facilitator

Purposeful and 'accidental' exposure to music helps people to develop musically. A Japanese study of people with little or no formal musical training who regularly partook in karaoke in their free time demonstrated the acquisition of specific highly developed musical skills (Mito, 2004). Whilst it may not be through karaoke, you will also have developed a wide range of musical skills over your life span.

Perhaps you are starting to realise that your own musical 'being' is more developed and extensive than you might have originally thought. What about your general confidence as a teacher, and your ability to engage and motivate pupils in your class? Where, when and how do you feel most comfortable with this and how can music build on this? The following task, which is used to help you think about yourself as a music teacher, is also the basis of a formative assessment strategy used in Chapter 8.

TASK 1.4

This task encourages you to think about:

(a) your own current perception of the constructs of an excellent teacher of music in the primary school classroom

(b) your own self-rating in relation to these constructs.

1. Use a polar graph paper with 8 segments and 10 concentric circles (Figure 1.2). Around the outside of the chart, write down up to 8 constructs you think would make an excellent teacher of music in your primary school setting (one by each segment). It is likely that some of these will be generic aspects of an excellent teacher, whilst some may be more specifically related to music teaching.

For example, you might feel that you want to include:

Flexible

Inclusive

Confident

This 'performance profile exercise' (Butler and Hardy, 1992) is based on the 'theory of personal constructs' (Kelly, 1955); it is not seeking 'right' answers; your own views are centrally important.

2. Next, you will need to consider each of these constructs in turn and think about what the polar opposite would be. In the examples above:

3. inflexible————————————flexible

4. exclusive————————————inclusive

5. no confidence————————————extremely confident

6. With 0 on the centre of each segment and 10 on the outside, you should decide how you would rate yourself against each of the constructs and colour in the appropriate amount of segments. For example, if you rate yourself as 3 out of 10 on the 'flexibility' scale, you should colour in the first three blocks moving out from the centre of the chart. Whilst you may wish to share this chart with someone else, this chart is for you only; there is no point in not being honest with yourself.

7. Once the chart is complete, look at the representation of yourself as a music teacher, celebrate the strengths and then set three targets for development.

These should be SMART (Specific, Measurable, Action-based, Realistic and Time-related) – perhaps two goals for the next term and one longer-term goal to be achieved over the rest of the academic year. Write these on the sheet – first, this will help you to remember them, and second, targets that are written down are more likely to be adhered to (Wanlin et al., 1997).

8. Now think about and write down some practical strategies for helping you to achieve these targets. For example, who will you talk to, observe, ask? What will you read? Where and when will you try out instruments? How will you develop your own confidence to sing?

9. Keep this chart and refer to it periodically. At the end of the term/year, update the chart in relation to how you feel about yourself as a teacher of music.

Hopefully, you are starting to realise that there is a lot you already know and can do. The question now is how to capitalise on and develop this in your classroom to bring to life the kinds of engaging, relevant and enjoyable musical experiences that you and your class want to have.

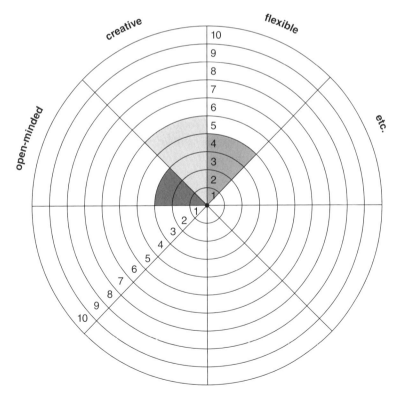

Figure 1.2 Example radar chart – constructs of an excellent music teacher

---

TASK 1.5

Write down on individual pieces of paper any personal hang-ups about teaching music. What is it that really bothers you? What are the stumbling blocks?

On paper of a different colour, write down all the things you are good at, things that you know and can build on. Think about what inspires you musically and write this down too.

Over the course of the book, keep this list in mind and revisit it frequently as your teaching develops.

Chapter summary

From reading this chapter, hopefully you now recognise the value you bring to children's already rich and constantly developing musical lives and can begin to understand the myriad of ways in which music and learning evolve. This chapter shines a lens on you, encouraging you to explore your thoughts and feelings about music education in a fast-changing world, to think about the things which you are good at and to acknowledge anything that may make you nervous about teaching music. Examining these aspects hopefully provides opportunities for you to consider your views on the purpose, value and importance of education more broadly, and to begin to consider where music education fits into this. Bass player Victor Wooten (2013) describes some important ideas about musical learning and encourages us to let children 'jam' with others, rather than treat musical learning as special or different. Wooten's point is that we wouldn't tell children they can only hold conversations with other children with a similar level of vocabulary and command of language, so why do we often try to impose this within a music education environment?

Your influence on children's musical learning is your indelible footprint – the content, order and way in which it is presented and experienced, the assessment and the evaluation of success, what is in, what is out – are all decided by you. Taking ownership and responsibility for your ideas helps develop understanding and value. Shying away from teaching music will leave no footprint whatsoever, which is a disaster.

Further reading

Pitts, S. (2012) *Chances and Choices: Exploring the Impact of Music Education*. Oxford: Oxford University Press.

Resources

Expert Subject Advisory Group (2013–14) New Music Curriculum Guidance. Available at: https://sites.google.com/site/newmusiccurriculumguidance/

Wooten, V. (2013) Music as a Language. Ted talk, 29 May. Available at: www.youtube.com/watch?v=2zvjW9arAZ0

2

EXPLORING MUSICAL LEARNING

Learning can be considered as the process by which people acquire, understand, apply and extend knowledge, concepts, skills and attitudes. Children and young people also discover their feelings towards each other and towards learning itself. Learning is thus a combination of cognitive, social and affective elements. The teachers' recognition of what learners bring to their education is crucial. (Pollard et al., 2014: 34)

Introduction

This chapter explores some of the complexities of musical learning – what learning is, how and where we learn and how music in schools contributes to developing musicianship. Pollard et al.'s (2014) broad definition of learning demonstrates that music education potentially contributes to all of these processes. Yet music also goes beyond this; as Reimer (1989: 50) notes, it is the embodiment of music that sets it aside from other more mainstream subjects; that is, 'we receive an "experience of" feeling rather than "information about" feeling' – signifying the aesthetic.

Musical learning happens in a variety of settings. *The Music Manifesto* (DfES, 2005), the first of two reports outlining the then Labour government's commitment to music education, defined three 'sectors' of music education (Table 2.1). Children may engage in musical learning in all three sectors, even within a school environment.

Table 2.1 Music education sectors as defined by *The Music Manifesto*

Formal	Learning takes place in statutory provision or with statutory funding in schools, colleges or music services
Non-formal	Learning takes place outside formal education provision, but can include out-of-hours work in schools, supervised by adult professionals
Informal	Young people organise and lead learning themselves without adult supervision

Source: The Music Manifesto (DfES, 2005)

Fundamentally, learning needs to make children believe in themselves and develop as learners in ways that have currency and validity beyond the classroom and extend into the future, regardless of where learning takes place.

Objectives

Through this chapter you will:

- explore ideas about how and where musical learning happens
- consider what musical learning is
- identify barriers and enablers to learning.

Exploring musical learning

When thinking of 'a musician', we likely head straight to a vision of someone actually 'doing it' – making and/or creating music, which is probably what children want from music education. Music learning is practical and experiential – learning through doing and through the experience of immersion in music. As Paynter (1982: xiii) notes in his guiding principles for music education, 'Music is a way of listening to sounds, and musical experience is a way of working with sounds and learning to control the medium'.

A collation of the Statutory Framework for the Early Years Foundation Stage (EYFS) curriculum (DfE, 2014a) and the National Curriculum for Music (DfE, 2013) yields a model given in Table 2.2. Note, however, that the learning outlined combines activities, behaviours, attitudes and outcomes. These are not intended to be seen as a cumulative progression; such an additive approach is misleading as learning is not always linear.

Table 2.2   Music education as defined within the EYFS and the National Curriculum for Music

EYFS Ages 3-5	Key Stage 1 (ages 5-7)	Key Stage 2 (ages 7-11)
explore and play with a wide range of media and materials	use technology appropriately	
	have the opportunity to learn a musical instrument	
	play tuned and untuned instruments musically	play and perform in solo and ensemble contexts, using their voices and playing musical instruments with increasing accuracy, fluency, control and expression
investigate and experience things and 'have a go'		
concentrate	listen with discrimination	
	listen with concentration and understanding to a range of high-quality live and recorded music	listen with attention to detail and recall sounds with increasing aural memory

EYFS Ages 3-5	Key Stage 1 (ages 5-7)	Key Stage 2 (ages 7-11)
keep on trying if they encounter difficulties	increase their self-confidence, creativity and sense of achievement	
have and develop their own ideas, make links between ideas and develop strategies for doing things	create and compose music on their own and with others	
	experiment with, create, select and combine sounds using the inter-related dimensions of music	improvise and compose music for a range of purposes using the inter-related dimensions of music
sing songs, make music and dance, and experiment with ways of changing them.	learn to sing and to use their voices	
	use their voices expressively and creatively by singing songs and speaking chants and rhymes	develop an understanding of musical composition, organising and manipulating ideas within musical structures and reproducing sounds from aural memory
safely use and explore a variety of materials, tools and techniques, experimenting with colour, design, texture, form and function		
children use what they have learnt about media and materials in original ways, thinking about uses and purposes. They represent (and share) their own ideas, thoughts and feelings through design and technology, art, music, dance, role-play and stories.	creativity	
	engage and inspire pupils to develop a love of music	
	develop a critical engagement with music	
		use and understand staff and other musical notations
	listen with discrimination to the best in the musical canon	
	develop their talent as musicians	
	appreciate and understand a wide range of high-quality live and recorded music drawn from different traditions and from great composers and musicians	
		develop an understanding of the history of music.

Source: Compiled from EYFS (DfE, 2014a) and the National Curriculum for Music (DfE, 2013)

The language used by the EYFS framework leans towards experiential learning, having a go, acting creatively and developing what might be considered as essential habits for learning – resilience, experimentation, personal discovery, learning through experience, etc. It also embraces aesthetic possibilities, for example sharing thoughts and feelings about music. In contrast, the limited guidance within the Key Stage 1 and 2 National Curriculum documentation focuses on a broad set of activities and outcomes in which listening, composing and performing are more clearly delineated as artificially separate entities and a body of knowledge is assumed.

The inherent principles of the EYFS framework are useful in helping to bring the National Curriculum for Key Stages 1 and 2 to life. The holistic approaches are underpinned by Paynter's (1982: xiii) guiding principles, including 'making music is more important than musical information – which is only a support for musical activity'. The *integral* relationship between making music, creating music and being critically engaged as a performer, composer and listener, has synergy with the approaches advocated throughout this book.

Musical knowledge

Current educational policy focuses attention on 'knowledge', a central facet of the increasingly prevalent neoliberal educational policies evolving in the UK and elsewhere throughout all levels of education (Allsup, 2015). In initial teacher education, a 'subject knowledge audit' examining 'subject matter knowledge' and 'knowledge of teaching the subject' (pedagogical content knowledge), is often central.

However, knowledge is a complex term, defined in multiple ways. As Wright (2012: 23) candidly notes:

> Knowledge that finds its way into schools as the music curriculum is never neutral. It is the result of ideologically impregnated policy through which it becomes filtered to enhance and preserve the culture and economic interests of the dominant social group. As such, it is a relay for certain social and cultural values.

Table 2.3 breaks down one way of defining knowledge types, relating these specifically to musical learning.

Table 2.3   Examples of types of knowledge displayed through musical learning

Knowledge type	Example
Knowledge 'about'	Knowing the significance of the lyrics in relation to the story Knowing that the song has a call and response structure in the chorus Knowing that many songs have verses and choruses Knowing the meaning of the term 'descending'
Knowledge 'how'	How to sing and change the pitch of your voice How to play with other people How to project your voice How to sing and do actions simultaneously How to pitch the first note from hearing the backing track

Knowledge type	Example
Knowledge 'of'	Knowing that changing your voice gives rise to different sounds Knowing that when the conductor lifts their hands, you should be ready to play Knowing that the shape of melodies goes up and down Knowing that some notes are longer than others

Source: adapted from Philpott, 2016

Here is a classroom example of different types of knowledge interweaving through musical learning:

> Year 2 pupils, dressed as shepherds, perform a catchy, upbeat song in the school's annual nativity to a packed intergenerational family audience. Singing along to a backing track, they add simple actions (which they agreed in a lesson) including stamping, clapping and pointing, 'painting' the lyrics with their gestures.
>
> The chorus includes a 'call and response' section; one group asks the question 'what are you looking for?' and the others respond 'we're looking for a baby'. The children learnt this song in a number of ways – from an audio recording playing in the background as they entered the classroom each morning and changing for PE over the previous three weeks, by rote (copying a line at a time) from the teacher, and from playing musical games such as laying out the shape of the phrase 'what are you looking for' with coloured counters, noting the descending pattern.

Yet, Reid (1967: 131) warns us that by reducing musical learning to an exclusive focus on certain knowledge types, we overlook 'embodiment' – a fundamental dimension of the arts:

> In the art-experience of the whole person, the body and mind together, the bodily side is important in ways in which it is not important, say, in mathematical or in scientific thinking. In our total contemplative absorption in art the quality of our own embodied living through it is enhanced. It is an experience which is intrinsically valuable, good for its own sake, a raising of the level of psycho-physical being.

In planning music lessons and musical learning experiences, we need to be mindful that by focusing exclusively on developing skills, understanding and knowledge, embodiment and aesthetic knowing may be unwittingly being sidelined.

The knowledge and understanding that we acquire through 'musicianship' is complex, and contextually bound. Elliott (2014: 1) notes the following:

> Musicianship, which *includes* listenership, is a rich form of procedural knowledge that draws upon four other *kinds* of musical knowing in surrounding and supporting ways. Musicianship is context-sensitive, or situated: that is, the precise nature and content of musicianship and listenership differs from musical practice to practice ... Musicianship is a form of cognition – a rich form of thinking and knowing – that is educable and applicable to all.

Combining diverse thoughts on knowledge and the philosophy of knowledge, on which this book has only scratched the surface, we begin to understand the all-encompassing potential impact of a musical education – mind, body and soul.

Models of learning

An understanding of how we think and learn has the potential to impact on the way in which learning is designed (Wood, 1998). Sloboda's (2005) work explores a series of interlocking areas relating to musical learning – cognitive processes of learning, the impact of motivation, talent and skill development, and the function and existence of music in the real world, in which values underpin experiences. Sloboda's model highlights many kinds of learning – from that which is deliberately sought, such as deliberate repetitive practice of a specific skill, to learning primarily developed through interactive social processes as we go about our everyday life.

Bloom et al. (1956) propose a model of three inter-related domains of learning – *thinking* (cognitive domain), *feeling* (affective domain) and *doing* (psychomotor/kinaesthetic domain). All of these are important in music, and applicable both in and out of school.

Cognitive learning is perhaps the best-known domain in Bloom et al.'s (1956) 'Taxonomy of Educational Objectives'. In this taxonomy, knowledge and understanding progressively develop as we move from simple cognitive functions such as recall, towards bringing together multiple ideas and sources in order to critique, justify and evaluate. This system of classification, which assumes a hierarchical structure through which 'higher order' thinking and deeper learning can be developed, has undergone many adaptations and revisions.

However, the taxonomy can be useful in thinking about ways of developing and supporting learning. For a critical examination of this issue, see Fautley's (2010) book *Assessment in Music Education*.

TASK 2.1

Look at the potential activities in Table 2.4 and identify those you would consider useful for developing musical learning.

The activities in the left column suggest 'knowledge of' music, for example the instruments of the orchestra and the position of notes on a stave. However, these could be better developed through acquiring this 'knowledge' from more inherently musical activities, encouraging pupils to act and think musically. Teachers need to know their pupils well in order to be able to develop questions and tasks offering appropriate challenge.

Table 2.4   Examples of lower- and higher-order thinking

Activities engaging lower-order thinking	Activities engaging higher-order thinking
• Repeated rehearsal of a musical phrase • Researching facts about composers • Memorising note names on the musical stave in isolation of sound • Copying down musical terms • Colouring in pictures of instruments • Chanting 'Every Good Boy Deserves Food' to learn the notes on the lines of the treble clef	• Repeated rehearsal and improvement of technique and fluency through own critical evaluation and reflective/reflexive action • Devising a plan for how to develop own music • Working out a basic melodic shape by ear • Comparing two versions of the same song • Creating a melody on a musical instrument or using technology • Working out which of four graphic representations accurately represents the musical phrase heard

Metacognition and self-regulation

There is often a need for repetition in order to make improvements (e.g. when learning to fluently play a musical phrase on the xylophone), which, on the one hand, could be considered a low-order thinking skill. However, since the ambition with such an activity is to develop the quality somehow – perhaps the fluency, tone, timing or technique – cognitive engagement at a higher level is required in order to recognise what needs changing through self-critique, working out how to adapt, trying it out, and keeping on going through this cycle. This kind of cycle is the essence of *metacognition* – a crucial set of learning skills bringing together awareness of the knowledge of cognition and the skills of self-regulation. Metacognition is described by the DfES thinking skills group (no date, cited in Fautley and Savage, 2007: 39) as 'the process of planning, assessing and monitoring one's own thinking ... thinking about thinking in order to develop understanding or self-regulation'. As Claxton (1999: 21) states, 'learning to learn is knowing when, how and what to do when you don't know what to do', an adaptation of an idea first used by Piaget to describe intelligence. This is different from just 'learning', which Claxton (1999: 21) describes as 'what you do when you don't know what to do'.

Self-regulation is defined by Vohs and Baumeister (2004: 2) as 'any efforts by the human self to alter any of its own inner states or responses ... thoughts, emotions, impulses or appetites, task performances ... [and] attentional processes'.

McPherson and Renwick's (2001) longitudinal study of musical development reports that when learning a musical instrument, the level and quality of self-regulation varies in line with skill. Between the ages of 7 and 9 years, they suggest that self-regulation in general is low, thereby proposing that it develops over time, possibly as a function of maturation, environmental or skill-level factors or a combination of these. They conclude that the main priority in skill development is to provide learners with the means by which they can develop their own learning strategies to enable them to focus their practice time and concentration, recommending that children are given the encouragement to self-monitor, set goals and evaluate their actions to assist their skill development. The development of these abilities leads to self-regulatory strategies becoming automatised later in a child's development and is beneficial to subsequent skill advancement (Macnamara and Collins, 2009).

These recommendations are important when you are planning learning experiences for your class.

TASK 2.2

Think about a music lesson you taught or observed recently:

1. Were there examples within the learning situation which encouraged the development of higher-order thinking skills? If so, were these successful and how do you know?

2. Was there a focus on self-regulation in any way? If so, how was this achieved?

3. How would you adapt the lesson to cognitively engage pupils more effectively?

Affective learning encompasses the development of our thoughts, interests, behaviours, attitudes, values and the social-emotional aspects of learning. In music, there are many ways in which these are important; examples are given in Table 2.5. Evidently, self-regulation transcends affective learning and overlaps partially with cognitive learning. Sheridan (1991: 29) argues that affective objectives of learning are of fundamental importance, since they are required to help pupils 'gain positive self-concept, greater self-esteem and a more developed sense of competency'. This needs to happen from a young age, since it is clear that early experiences can impact on children in the future. This is particularly important if children are to remain motivated to be involved in music education.

Table 2.5 Examples of affective learning through music education

- Having an emotional response to a piece of music; responding to music in ways which reflect own thoughts and feelings
- Controlling emotions in socially acceptable ways during a rehearsal when working with others
- Handling anxiety and nerves etc. during a performance
- Communicating with an audience through music
- Not giving up when things are not right instantly
- Feeling confident to join in and that the learning/task is achievable
- Valuing music lessons in school

All of the examples in Table 2.5 are important for developing musicianship and creativity. Through music education, we strive to develop habits and behaviours that allow us to develop as musicians. For example, if we don't play something as desired on the first attempt and then give up, it will be difficult to develop some aspects of musicianship. Likewise, if we don't have the willingness or the confidence to try out our own ideas when composing, or we can't work with other people, learning is likely to be affected.

Psychomotor learning is the third domain of Bloom et al.'s (1956) taxonomy. This encompasses the development of motor skills and manual skills. According to Krathwohl et al. (1964, cited in Miller et al., 1998: 69), psychomotor learning relates to aspects which 'emphasize some muscular or motor skill, some manipulation of material and objects, or some act which requires neuro-muscular co-ordination'.

Simpson (1971) further develops these ideas into a model with differing levels of classification, following the same structure as the design of the cognitive and affective domains. There is much potential for the development of psychomotor skills in music education, particularly through the development of instrumental, vocal and technological skills. Physical maturity plays a part in this development. As before, this domain of learning inter-relates to the cognitive and affective domains. Table 2.6 offers some potential examples of psychomotor learning.

Table 2.6   Examples of psychomotor learning in music education

- Hearing that a recording has 'jammed'
- Listening to the sound of a G string on another pupil's ukulele and then tuning the G string on own instrument through pitch matching
- Adjusting the volume of own instrument or voice to blend in with others
- Watching conductor and stopping when directed
- Practising striking individual notes on a xylophone
- Trying out different sounds on a tambourine
- Singing with expression and stylistic awareness
- Improving the fluency and accuracy of a musical phrase through repetition
- Creating music based on a given or chosen starting point
- Arranging the pre-recorded loops on a tablet computer application to create a simple repeating chord sequence

TASK 2.3

Look back through the previous tables of examples of cognitive and affective learning.
    Identify which of the activities listed in these also require psychomotor learning in order to be successful.
    What does this tell you about the domains of learning?

Spiral learning models

Bamberger (2006: 71) states that: 'Musical development is enhanced by continuously evolving interactions among multiple organizing constraints along with the disequilibrium and sensitivity to growing complexity that these entanglements entrain.'

This points towards a spiral model of development, in which knowledge, skills and understanding are constantly learnt, consolidated, revised and developed on a series of inter-related planes. Spiral models of learning are well established (e.g. Bruner, 1960, 1975). In terms of music specifically, Swanwick and Tillman (1986) proposed a sequence of musical development around a study of children's compositions based on Piaget's Stage Development Model. Similarly, Thomas (1970) produced a spiral model following the Manhattanville Music Curriculum Project, which was concerned with children's rejection of school music as they reached Piaget's 'logic and reasoning' stage. It focused on three areas of relevance: artistic, personal and social. Whilst this is arguably more applicable to older children, towards the end of the primary phase there is evidence of children clearly delineating music in school and music out of school (e.g. Lamont et al., 2003; Marshall and Hargreaves, 2007) and is something we should be mindful of when planning musical learning.

The importance of motivation

Children need to be drawn into learning and motivated to want to get involved. The topic of motivation is a whole area of study you may wish to explore further, but within the confines of this book we can only scratch the surface.

Historically, it seems that academic researchers have not been particularly good at asking children directly about their views, but have instead made many judgements on what we assume they think. This is highlighted by Smith et al. (2005) who carried out a systematic review of what 11–16-year-olds believed motivated them to learn. Of 13,730 articles screened for suitability, only eight were selected for in-depth case studies through meeting the inclusion criteria. Of these, only one came from music. Many others were rejected because they were about children's motivation but completely ignored children's own perspectives.

The findings offer multiple ways in which music teaching in primary school could benefit, including considerations of planning or content, organisation of learning, engagement, values, assessment ownership, relevance and autonomy. Table 2.7 brings together Smith et al.'s (2005: summary) results and makes suggestions for implementation within music education. The degree of overlap between these categories should be noted.

There are significant challenges to motivating all pupils at all times and there are times when we have to accept that some children cannot be fully motivated for a range of reasons. Often, though, there are ways in which motivation can be improved in order to re-engage someone in learning, if only temporarily.

Table 2.7 Factors impacting motivation for musical learning

Category	Considerations within school music education
The role of self	• Multiple factors influence pupils' decisions about music in school, and once made, these decisions become the dominant influence on levels of engagement: ○ Your 'teacher radar' needs to always be scanning in order to be aware of the influences and to do what you can to support pupils; these influences come from a range of places and people – friends, parents, siblings, other teachers (including instrumental teachers), popular culture, events in school, as well as the curriculum itself, the way learning is promoted and the impact of 'assessment' if not used well • Children prefer to work in groups; group work increases engagement • Teacher expectations impact on motivation; teachers need to show all pupils that they have high expectations which are realistic and motivating
Utility	Learning needs to be perceived as useful and relevant. In terms of music, this should include: • bringing in children's own musical preferences and ideas • encouraging them to bring instruments they play into class music lessons to use within the curriculum • building links between what children are familiar with and where you want to take them • helping children to be able to feel that their 'real' musical self can be developed in school, rather than creating divisions between school music and 'real' music
Pedagogy	• Pupils prefer activities that are fun, collaborative, informal and active – this should be central to the decisions made when planning and teaching • The teacher's attitude affects pupils' engagement. The messages and signals you send out about how you feel about pupils need to be positive and encouraging. Some teachers may be feeling under-confident to teach music, but should really make an effort to join in and act musically, modelling where appropriate, rather than being detached from the musical culture in the lesson • Authentic learning tasks are more likely to engage pupils cognitively, so helping them to recognise the purpose of the learning and see the relevance beyond just a task in a lesson is important
The influence of peers	• It is important not to be made to appear foolish in front of the peer group. Some children may be shy or embarrassed to perform or answer questions in front of others. Teachers should get to know their pupils as quickly as possible and work hard to create a safe and creative classroom environment where risk taking is encouraged • How groups are organised needs careful consideration and is likely to vary from situation to situation. Think about ways to bring together children from different social groups and different ages – music is fantastically flexible to be able to include children and adults with different skill levels and experiences

(Continued)

Table 2.7 (Continued)

Category	Considerations within school music education
Learning	• Pupils believe that effort is important and can make a difference; they are influenced by the expectations of teachers and the wider community • Expectations should be high, offer appropriate challenge and be achievable; individual and collective successes should be valued and celebrated

Curriculum	• A curriculum can isolate pupils from their peers and from the subject matter. This needs careful and considered planning to overcome – you may also be able to bring pupils into some of the curriculum decision making in order to have an evolving and co-constructed curriculum. Think about what is in your curriculum and why – is it the right thing for these particular pupils?
	• Some pupils believe the curriculum is restricted in what it recognises as achievement; assessment influences how pupils see themselves as learners and social beings:
	  o There is absolutely no need to give 'grades and marks' to pupils; using dialogic feedback in encouraging ways should help all children to move forward in their learning
	• The way that the curriculum is mediated can send messages that it is not accessible at all:
	  o Try to create a curriculum that has plenty of scope for all pupils to recognise that they are making progress, to celebrate everyone's achievements, and which takes account of what children want from music education
	  o Think about who is 'demonstrating' or performing – is it always the same pupils?
	  o If you were a pupil, do you think that you would pick up the values your teacher wishes to embody? Are they the right values? Are they fully inclusive? What would they say about your attitude in the classroom and your dual role as a teacher and a musician?

Source: adapted from Smith et al., 2005

TASK 2.4

Decide what you will do as the teacher in each of the scenarios below.

Ellie, a Year 5 pupil, is usually an engaged learner, taking a leading part in group work. She plays trumpet in the school band and is in the school street dance group. Today, Ellie is taking a very passive role in her group's attempts to improvise over a repeating chord pattern using the notes of a pentatonic scale (C, D, E, G and A). Looking around, you notice that the rest of the class seem to be enjoying themselves and engaged in the task.

In this situation, there may be a multitude of reasons why Ellie is unmotivated to join in. Here are a few – think about each situation in turn and consider what actions you might take to help Ellie re-engage:

---

1. Ellie's mother died recently; this is her first day back at school after the funeral.

2. Ellie does not like playing tuned percussion instruments.

3. Ellie perceives the task to be too easy – she attempted it initially and then gave up over the perceived lack of challenge.

4. Ellie fell out with her friend at lunchtime, directly before this lesson.

5. Ellie has just stopped learning the trumpet. Free provision in the school through a whole-class scheme has recently come to an end and Ellie's family is unable to pay for on-going lessons.

6. Ellie just got the result of her science test and had not done as well as her friends.

7. Ellie's best friend was chosen to help demonstrate with the teacher when the task was set.

8. Ellie is not entirely sure what she needs to do.

9. Ellie is a speaker of English as an additional language.

10. Ellie is too hot.

The list could go on and on. The point is that motivating all children is key to effective education. Situations, environments, relationships, moods and feelings are all dynamic and we are all different. Some children are motivated by competition, yet this makes other children switch off. Some come to school to escape their problems at home and are glad of the opportunities to immerse themselves in learning. Others cannot function effectively. We can adapt what we do, or the way we are, and it will hopefully make a difference. You need to keep trying so that children don't think you've given up on them, but there isn't always a magic solution that will draw someone into learning on a given day. Yet, as the list shows, there are plenty of things for us to reflect on to help us keep adapting what we do and how we do it, striving to motivate and engage everyone.

Barriers to engagement

There are many barriers to full participation that are more or less prevalent at any one time. You could think of these as being like a graphic equaliser – on some days, they may all be at zero or full, but on other days some issues may arise which prevent full engagement with musical (and other) learning.

Figure 2.1 (Daubney and Marshall, 2011) shows a model of identified barriers to musical learning/engagement for looked-after children who were offered the opportunity to take part in music 'taster sessions' as part of a summer holiday course. The categorisations are not mutually exclusive and there is a degree of overlap between some aspects.

Whilst some of the barriers were identified from children who engaged with the courses and were barriers they had overcome, there are many children who found

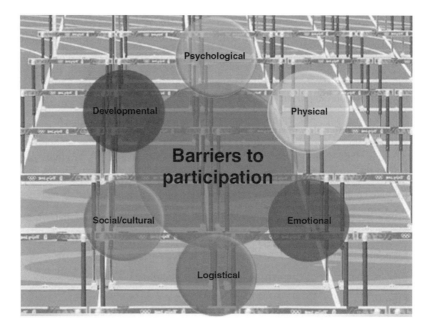

Figure 2.1 Barriers to participation in music for looked-after children

Source: Daubney and Marshall, 2011

Reprinted with collective permission from Rhythmic Music Charity, Brighton & Hove Music Trust, Brighton & Hove Music and Arts and the National Foundation for Youth Music

engagement difficult or impossible and were unable to overcome enough barriers for them to engage at all. Table 2.8 highlights specific examples of barriers affecting children of primary school age.

Ofsted (2012, 2013) notes that engagement in extra-curricular music is not always representative of a school's population, for example involving fewer children who have free school meals, who are from specific groups such as travellers or who are in care (looked-after children) than in the general school population. Whether or not children fall into a specific 'category', they can be difficult to engage and therefore a concerted, on-going effort is needed to encourage and include all children and for teachers to see past the 'labels' which may be attached to children.

TASK 2.5

Decide what would you do in the following situation:

Kelly, a Year 6 pupil with a love of singing, begins to draw attention to herself through poor behaviour manifested by shouting out and being disrespectful towards people and instruments towards the end of every music lesson.

Table 2.8   Examples of barriers to learning

Logistical	• Finance – affording lessons, clubs, trips • Getting forms signed by parents/carers • Getting to venues • Staying behind after school for rehearsals or concerts • Getting involved in lunchtime clubs when they need to queue for their free school meal • Family having no insurance so cannot take instruments home • Having no access to computers/instruments outside the classroom • Length of the sessions unsuitable to meet the needs of the individual
Emotional	• Difficulties forming relationships with others • Difficulty expressing feelings and emotions • Difficulty in handling the emotions evoked by some music and topics • Difficulty in understanding the boundaries of relationships with others • Inability to deal with emotions in large groups in socially acceptable ways • Finding the ending of 'projects' difficult, as they have formed a bond with a particular person
Social/cultural	• Difficulty working with other people in large groups • Wanting to choose who they work with outside of the classroom (e.g. not just other children who are 'labelled' with similar issues/difficulties) • Wanting to be with people who understand them • Not knowing what they are signing up for • Not having the confidence to get involved without their friends • Peer pressure – it is not 'cool'
Developmental	• Lack of challenge • Learning not broken down enough • Pace too fast • Inability to access learning through ways introduced • Inability to process instructions
Psychological	• Fear of failure • Reticence to try something new • Poor self-image • Low self-esteem • Low resilience • Being unable or unwilling to commit to more sustained work at that particular point in time • Difficulty engaging in learning both initially and on a sustained basis
Physical	• Learning not being adapted to help engage pupils appropriately with learning or medical disabilities or issues • Inability to access the learning space • Physical dexterity issues

Source: adapted from Daubney and Marshall, 2011

This is what actually happened:

> The music teacher kept Kelly behind at the end of the lesson for three consecutive weeks. During these short, 5-minute sessions with the music teacher, it became quickly apparent that Kelly was purposely misbehaving to gain exclusive attention from the teacher. Advice was sought from the class teacher, revealing that Kelly was the youngest of five children. As each of the older siblings had reached the age of 11, they had been placed into foster care. Kelly was coming up to her 11th birthday and had severe anxiety issues impacting on her behaviour, her confidence and her need for one-to-one attention. Knowing a little more about Kelly's situation helped the music teacher to rebuild a little of Kelly's confidence by using the 5 minutes at the end of the lesson to work with Kelly and a chosen friend on something that the class would be doing in the next lesson in order to help her feel confident to participate effectively. The music teacher also invited a support assistant into a lesson to join in for the last 15 minutes. This helped Kelly recognise that there was a network of people in the school who could support her emotionally and also celebrate her achievements.

Fear of failure

According to Claxton (2002: 17), creative learners display many desirable qualities, including being 'ready, willing and able to work in different ways' and developing resilience, both of which are related to risk taking. Some children feel that it is better not to do something than to 'fail' at it. There are aspects of our education system that perpetuate this. For example, if children feel that school is about seeking 'right' answers, it must be confusing when a teacher says 'try something out' or 'experiment with the sounds'. Fear of failure manifests itself in the classroom in many different ways, for example from a child who quietly does not take part to the 'class clown' who successfully avoids doing something by averting attention. In order to help children overcome their fear of failure, we need to help them have the motivation and self-determination to 'have a go'.

Conroy et al. (2002: 77) identified five main fears of failure in sport:

1. Fear of experiencing shame and embarrassment
2. Fear of devaluing one's self-estimate
3. Fear of having an uncertain future
4. Fear of losing social influence/fear of important others losing interest
5. Fear of upsetting important others

Clearly, there is much synergy between the reasons for fear of failure in sport and those relevant to music education. It is important for teachers to be aware of the potential for fear of failure when planning and implementing learning opportunities. According to Sagar et al. (2009: 75):

> Fears are generally accepted as normative during childhood and are considered as an adaptive emotional reaction to threat (real or imagined). Fears are an adaptive aspect of development that warn one of dangers and motivate escape or avoidance behaviour.

Humans are complicated beings with complex and dynamic needs, behaviours and thoughts. Returning to the analogy of the graphic equaliser, it is important that teachers put in the time and effort to get to know their pupils as human beings and not just as classroom music students. Whilst on the one hand I sometimes hear that teachers or visiting artists do not want to know anything about pupils before they meet them for the first time so that they do not have negative preconceptions, I personally think this is a rather short-sighted attitude. After all, how do you expect to provide worthwhile, motivating and appropriately challenging learning if you do not know enough about the people you are personalising it for?

Chapter summary

This chapter has explored multiple ideas about how, where and when children learn, as well as considering barriers and enablers to learning. Learning is complex – it is impacted by situations, interactions, personalities, motivations, experiences, moods, feelings, emotions, cultures and much more. Some learning is deliberate, some is 'caught' through our engagement with the world and some is perhaps a combination of both. Returning to the opening quote from Pollard et al., we recognise learning as multi-dimensional and acknowledge different levels and functions of learning. Teachers need to make a considerable effort to get to know their pupils in order to work out what motivates them and how to nurture their musical lives in holistic and meaningful ways which develop children's individual and collective musical identities. Everyone has different rates and ways of learning, bringing different experiences and preferences to musical learning, wherever it happens. Planning for this creates challenges for teachers not least because children's self-determination needs to be encouraged. All children are unique and special; we should nurture and celebrate this diversity. We need to work hard to build positive relationships in enabling environments, helping children to feel confident to take steps towards developing musicianship both inside and outside the classroom and school.

Further reading

Daubney, G. and Daubney, A. (2017) *Performance Anxiety: A Practical Guide for Music Teachers*. London: Incorporated Society of Musicians. Available at: www.ism.org/perfor mance-anxiety-guide

Fautley, M. (2010) *Assessment in Music Education*. Oxford: Oxford University Press.

Ofsted (2009) Making More of Music: Improving the quality of music teaching (primary). Available at: http://webarchive.nationalarchives.gov.uk/20141124154759/http://www. ofsted.gov.uk/resources/making-more-of-music-improving-quality-of-music-teaching-primary [This is not the most recent Ofsted report on music education but it has some useful guidance on music lessons and musical learning in primary school.]

Reid, L.A. (1986) *Ways of Understanding and Education*. London: Heinemann Educational.

Swanwick, K. (1988) *Music, Mind and Education*. London: Routledge.

3

SINGING AND VOCAL DEVELOPMENT

Singing is a kind of thing people would like to hear. A song. A little tune with some words in the tune. I like singing very much because I have lovely tunes in my voice and I feel happy when I sing. (Heather, age 6)

Introduction

Singing in a mud bath at Glastonbury with 150,000 Coldplay fans – epic. Singing with your primary school class – forget it! But why? In our daily lives, we sing, hum, whistle out loud to songs on the radio, at festivals, at religious events, sporting fixtures and on many other occasions. Playgrounds are full of chants and songs embedded into often highly physical games from all around the world, being taught and learnt by children as they explore their social groups and identities (Marsh, 2009). We all have extensive and evolving playlists of songs, chants, melodies and fragments in our head built up from experiences throughout life. Singing and songs in the 'rest' of children's lives outside of school are ever present, whether individually or communally. It is possibly the most inclusive activity there is. Our voice is the instrument we carry with us everywhere we go; it is unique to each individual. If we seriously want to develop a singing culture we need to make it a normal part of the culture in school, building a community where singing is frequently enjoyed and where the whole school community of children and adults get involved.

Singing plays an important role in wellbeing for people of all ages (Clift et al., 2015). The feelings evoked from being part of, or even hearing, a large choir makes the hairs on the back of your neck stand up and is life-affirming. Our voice is unique to us, yet perhaps that is what causes a block for some people – it is a very personal part 'of us' in a way that a regular musical instrument isn't. Additionally, there are many examples of singers we admire – it is, after all, also a professional pursuit. We probably all know friends and family who are keen on karaoke or sing-along-a-musicals. Then there are the Saturday night TV singing competitions in which vocal prowess (and marketing potential?) is 'spotted' – usually young people destined for temporary stardom amid a plethora of people who are vaguely good or significantly worse, beamed across the world for our general entertainment. I often

wonder whether the raising up of just a few individuals on a pedestal in this way promotes a fear of singing in public for the general population as it perpetuates the idea that some of us have special talents whilst the rest of us don't. Alongside this, I also worry about the psychological impact of rejection, perceived failure and performance anxiety – all very important topics beyond the limited scope to mention them in this book.

Street's (2006) study of the habits of mothers singing to their babies found that all 100 mothers in her sample, which was drawn from a wide socio-economic group, sang to their babies frequently in their own homes, even though most of these mothers claimed not to have a singing voice. A central finding of this research confirmed that mothers sing to their children many times a day and for multiple reasons, using an eclectic range of repertoires and vocal styles, and that bonding with their baby was both a core driver and outcome. These early experiences help musical and other development, including social, emotional and linguistic, in many ways.

Incorporating a chapter on singing into this book might lead you to think that units of work should be organised around singing alone. This is not the case. Singing is beneficial across making and creating music, and not just as a separate entity to 'learn to sing songs'. We need to free ourselves from thinking that singing is just about recreating songs in the ways we are familiar with them. There is huge potential in songs and in our voice to adapt, personalise, create and have fun. You need to give yourself permission to experiment with material, modelling to pupils that they can do this too.

Whilst much of the focus in this particular chapter is on helping you explore ways to embed singing in your class, you should also be mindful of the possibilities of vocal work across the music curriculum, through other subjects and also more generally as part of classroom and school life, for example as a way to energise a class, to change the mood, to welcome people to the school and to sing together at points in a school day. 'Singing' is the catch-all term used throughout the chapter to describe a rich array of vocal sounds, techniques and possibilities.

Objectives

Through this chapter you will:

- explore singing and vocal development as part of a rounded music education
- find ways into using your own voice
- try out strategies for developing singing and vocal work in the classroom
- consider repertoire, occasion and purpose
- recognise factors that promote singing and consider practical ways to overcome barriers.

Singing as fundamental to musical learning

Singing is a key musical skill and tool, integral to developing musicianship and creativity. Typically, we might think of singing as describing the act of 'singing a song'. However, singing has considerable potential. For example, singing helps us to internalise music – useful when we are trying to play a musical instrument and learn either by ear or from notation. It helps us construct and deconstruct the relationship between different sounds and pitches (notes). Through singing, we can construct and deconstruct music, learning about how it is constructed and the so-called 'elements of music'. In particular, singing and vocalising are ways of getting music into and out of our heads. The following examples help explain some of these ideas (the figures in Roman numerals relate to the notated examples in Figure 3.1).

Scenario 1

The children in Year 4 are developing lyric-writing skills. In today's lesson, the children are setting words to a melody. Earlier in the lesson, they 'took a balloon for a walk', listening and reacting to the second movement of 'The Surprise Symphony' by Haydn. Following careful questioning and everyone writing down three words on Post-it notes about the images created in their mind, Miss Timerick invites the class to join in humming the melody. Miss Timerick then explains the task – to write their own lyrics for the melody. She takes one of her words and puts it in a sentence, and quietly sings the first line of her song out loud:

'Trolls and pixies everywhere, hiding underneath the chair'. (i)

The class applauds. Miss Timerick gives each table 2 minutes to work out a possible next line together. Walking around, she hears the class trying out words and humming the melody. At the end of the 2 minutes, she chooses Lindsey's group to share its example. The children sing out loud from the beginning:

'Trolls and pixies everywhere, hiding underneath the chair.

Grandpa Troll climbs up each stair, reaching for the tree-house!' (ii)

The class laughs and applauds and is invited to sing it back. The children discuss word setting and syllables, unpicking the group's example, before going on to create their own based on the array of words written down earlier in the lesson.

In this example, singing is used to get the melody 'into their heads' (internalising) in order to be able to use it for other purposes. Having listened, the pupils are able to remember and vocalise it, which helps them when setting their own lyrics to the melody. Singing is also their vehicle for sharing their ideas.

Scenario 2

The following lesson class begins with a 'singing numbers' game. The teacher plays the note C on the chime bar to find her starting pitch and then sings up and down the scale – the children copy: 1-2-3-4-5-4-3-2-1 (iii). She changes the combinations of the melody – 1-3-5-5-3-1 (iv), then 1-1-7-7-6-6-5 (v) (going down from the 'root note'). Miss Timerick praises the class and then sets a more difficult challenge. This time, she will only sing the notes to the word 'moo' and the class will sing back the numbers. She starts again with the same scalic melody and the class sing back: 1-2-3-4-5-4-3-2-1 (iii). The game goes on, with the class mostly maintaining accuracy. Then she slips in the opening of the 'Surprise Symphony' melody, singing 'staccato' (all notes short and detached). The class sing back: 1-1-3-3-5-5-3 (vi). Next phrase – she sings again, this time going below the middle C. Some children work out the numbering system, whilst others add in only the first part or vaguely sing along: 4-4-2-2-7-7-5 (vii). Miss Timerick repeats this again, and the third time she shows the numbers on her outstretched fingers.

Facilitated through singing and game playing, this activity brings together children's previous experiences of the melody, helping them to accurately pitch notes and then explore the relationship between different pitches. It will eventually help them work out the melody by ear on tuned percussion instruments in order to play as part of a class ensemble as it has been internalised and the relationship between notes of the melody explored. Through using a 'sound first' approach, notation is introduced and the sonic and written pitch relationship is examined. Also, the melody is used as a stimulus for a more creative task.

Scenario 3

Year 6 pupils Ingrid and Marie are working together to create a melody to accompany a film clip of the sinking Titanic. Miss Vallance listens to their conversation and observes them trying out melodies on the xylophone. Ingrid explains she has a melody in her head but can't play it. Miss Vallance suggests Ingrid sings the short melody out loud. She records the short melancholy-sounding melody on her mobile phone, plays it back and leads a discussion. Could it be a vocal melody, or do they want to play it on an instrument? What might the shape look like if it was drawn? They agree on a starting note of D and Miss Vallance wanders away, leaving the girls to work out Ingrid's short and haunting melody.

In this scenario, singing was an effective vehicle through which Ingrid could share her melody. Vocalising is a very important way for us to get melodies out of our head, especially when we may not yet have the technical skills to play them, or the analytical skills to work out how to play them. This example also serves as a reminder that we need to give children plenty of different strategies for sharing their own musical ideas. If we judge everything just by what we hear from them playing, we are likely to get a diminished view of their ideas and capabilities.

Finding our voice

Singing is perhaps not something people feel they were 'taught to do' – it is something that may have developed more informally. In our early lives, the rise and fall of our voices, emerging through crying and baby babble, lead into gradually more coherent speech and spontaneous singing. Young children use their voices to create and mimic sounds, singing along to well-known favourites or joining in with family and friends and translating the words heard into language they know. Their spontaneous voice play means they have far fewer inhibitions than older children and adults. Jessica, a

Figure 3.1   Notated musical examples from scenarios 1 and 2

Year 1 pupil, came up one break time, threw her arms around me and sang 'You can take me home again' – a song she apparently liked to listen to in the car. It was, in fact, *You can make me whole again* by Atomic Kitten, but who cares? She had found the joy of singing and made it 'her' song. Children spontaneously create their own songs, importing and adapting internalised sounds, speech, songs and melodies to create their own improvised adapted versions of songs (Barrett, 2006).

It is clear that 'confidence' is situationally bound – in the safe environment of the home, singing with and to our own small children is well within most adults' comfort zone, yet I know many early years settings and primary schools where not all staff are confident to sing with children in their classes. These same people seem perfectly happy using their voices in other ways though – making the voices of characters and puppets, reading out rhythmical poems, playing games where facial expressions are vocalised or 'playing' skipping and clapping games in the playground, despite all of these being inherently linked to singing. This exemplifies why we need to broaden our understanding of the term 'singing' and give ourselves permission to be creative when we 'sing'.

TASK 3.1

To help you explore your own voice and develop vocal confidence, sing at least one song through out loud every day in the privacy of your own space. Over time, try out different types of songs and be brave with your voice. Experiment away. After all, the only person who can hear it is you!

As with all aspects of music, the creation of a musical community, in which teachers and children are all involved, is crucial. It is very difficult to convince children that singing is for everyone if they do not see us doing what we are asking them to do through our own regular active engagement, and instead merely 'tell' children what to do without adding our own voice. This means that teachers need to develop their own confidence, recognising and acknowledging that singing is a natural everyday activity for people of all ages and from all walks of life. We could also help children to recognise this through taking them into situations in communities where others sing and share their songs, from shopping centres to old people's homes.

Ways into singing seem best served through inclusive activities in which there is a critical mass of sound through which a 'have-a-go' ethos is adopted in a safe environment. Singing thrives in conditions where it is regularly undertaken, encouraging, inclusive, and recognises the need to bring children's musical worlds together. One school I know does this by having a community sing-song in the hall on a Friday morning before school. It invites everyone in – mums, dads, cleaners, teaching assistants, childminders, toddlers, babies, teachers and children. According to the attendance register, more children come to school on a Friday than any other day of the week. Is that just a coincidence?

The most important part of singing in primary school and early years settings is actually doing it. The technical aspects such as having a good posture and working on breathing are obviously important, yet secondary to the actual activity of singing. This is all technical stuff that you can develop once you are inside the music. After all, we don't check our posture when driving the car prior to belting out our favourite rock ballads along to the radio. Vocal health is important but much of this is common sense; for example, singing within achievable and sensible vocal ranges, not over-straining our vocal chords, warming up and warming down our voices, and drinking plenty of water. Along with the aforementioned potential teacher confidence issues, you need to be mindful that pupils may also lack the confidence to try things out vocally for many reasons, including shyness, lack of self-belief, fear of failure, fear of what their voice will sound like or others hearing it and vocal change due to physiological development, particularly for boys as their voices move increasingly towards maturity. Motivation is also important – consider these two scenarios and decide which one you would rather be part of as a pupil.

Scenario 4

The Year 5 class enters the room after break time to the track *Happy* by Pharrell Williams playing out loud. The children start to join in with sections of the lyrics, smiling and laughing with their friends and mime-playing instruments heard on the recording. Mr Williams fades the track and joins the pupils in the circle formation, made following his instructions given by the door. Mr Williams points to himself and starts off a vocal warm-up chanting from a poem, copied by the children when he points to them:

Make a little ball, push it round the ground;
All the children are cheering.
Sticks and twigs, carrots and stones;
A snowman starts appearing.

Throughout, Mr Williams shifts his weight from one foot to the other in time to the pulse of the rhyme, adapting his voice, changing the pitch of words high and low; changing the dynamics (volume), speaking in an array of different voices ('like the Queen' or 'like a robot'), and the class copies. After the second time through this chanting, Mr Williams proceeds to sing one phrase – 'Make a little ball, push it round the ground', over-accentuating the words. The class copies. And so it goes on: learning the song by rote, copying one line at a time, then two lines and eventually the whole chorus, accompanied by moving feet and hand actions. There is no break in the flow of the music through all this time and Mr Williams makes his breath intake obvious by indicating with his hand as he inhales.

Scenario 5

Year 5, waiting for the music lesson to begin, queues up in silence by the door. Mr Thomas invites them into the room to stand in a circle; the class dutifully obeys. Not a whisper. Mr Thomas starts the formalities of the lesson: 'Stand up straight. Let's all breathe in together and then out for the count of six. Who can remember what we need to use when we are trying to get air into the lungs? Hands up. OK, here we go again. We'll exhale for the count of six and keep adding one to see how far we can get.' The class completes this exercise and Mr Thomas continues: 'Today, we're going to learn a new song. I will say a line and then you repeat it.' The class begins to learn the song by rote; after 2 lines Mr Thomas stops again and says he is disappointed in the lack of clarity in the words. The children try again. Again, he stops the flow of the music and asks them to show where they are breathing in; this starts a conversation about whether they need to take a breath every line or whether every two lines would be better.

In both examples, the song is eventually learnt and the technical details are also considered, albeit in different ways and with this being a more explicit focus in scenario 5. In scenario 4, the class is more immersed and involved in a musical experience – the children's voices warm up and a new repertoire is learnt through on-going musical flow without considerable starting and stopping. Ultimately, this probably makes scenario 4 more motivating for pupils as they are actively involved in music for more sustained periods of time and the musical results of this approach are relatively quick and gratifying.

There is much you could do with this material to develop it. For example, what is the character of the snowman? What does he see in his imagination? Different groups could create their own rapped or sung verses and it could all be added together to create a class song with a shared chorus. Singing does not have to mean 'singing someone else's music'. Think back to the earlier examples of pre-school children spontaneously inventing their own songs. This is a natural extension.

Warming up the voice

Warm-up exercises wake up our vocal chords and also improve the quality of our vocal production. They also help to focus attention and give opportunities for developing specific musical and vocal skills. There are literally hundreds of warm-up songs and games to try out and have fun with – these do not all have to be exclusively in music lessons – indeed, they are a great way to get to know your class well at the beginning of the year and to re-focus attention during the school day. Vocal warm-ups might also involve moving the facial muscles and using voices in different ways to make sound effects or producing particular vocal sounds, chanting or many other vocal acrobatics. Warm-ups can also contribute to the development of a specific skill that is a main focus in a lesson, for example developing the articulation of words when singing or rapping, listening to each other in order to be more 'together', develop breathing, getting some melodic jumps more accurate, blending voices or staying in time and in tune. Remember also that many singing warm-ups will also include physical movements. This is great; in life, there is no clear distinction between music and movement. As with learning songs and singing, there are many musical 'games', for example parachute games that children love to play, where they sing without it being a main focus as the game playing distracts them.

TASK 3.2

Find and try out three vocal warm-ups in the safety of your own home. Decide which age group you would use the warm-up with. If you are feeling confident enough, try it out with a group or class.

Other teachers are likely to have ideas that you can use and adapt – for example, drama teachers often use warm-up games involving singing, chanting and physical movement.

Repertoire

> Children's musical preferences deserve to be acknowledged ... as this is the repertoire in which they are already steeped; it is part of their selfhood, their own identity. Their music may warrant inclusion in a class session, lesson or program. As we plan for our lessons and learning experiences with them, we must understand something of children's musical selves. We need to know them in order to teach them and to acknowledge and validate them through recognition of who they musically are. (Campbell, 1998: 201)

Repertoire choice is crucial and is often a factor in whether or not children are excited and motivated by singing. Remember, though, that not all of the song choices need to be yours – you could (and should) also include ideas from children. Ideally, material will be a combination of songs children know and additional new repertoire in a range of different styles and from different cultures, times and places, with a view to expanding children's aural sound bank and musical experiences. There are many different purposes for singing and times when you might sing and the repertoire will vary with the context; for example, singing for pleasure at the end of the day, a repertoire related to a particular theme for an assembly or a learning purpose, for a warm-up or an informal concert somewhere. How repertoire relates to a unit of work and what you plan to do with the music apart from singing it are also important factors.

There are a number of crucial things to consider when choosing a repertoire, whether for singing or another purpose:

- *What do you want to get out of it musically?* Specific music learning will often be the key purpose, for example to develop simple part-singing, to develop accuracy of intervals beyond notes that are next to each other, or to explore beat-boxing sounds. If all repertoire is chosen just for the lyrical content (e.g. to fit in with a topic on the dinosaurs), the focus of the learning may be lost, therefore knowing what you musically want from the lesson is the most important starting point. Deconstructing musical phrases is a very useful way to help children understand many aspects of music, developing and honing skills and techniques.
- *How is Part-singing developed?* Moving a group towards simple part-singing through rounds and partner songs (two or more songs sung at the same time)

and simple harmonies is experience, not age, dependent. In some schools, this is well established by the end of Year 2, whereas in others, it will be a year or two later.

- *Are the musical challenges of the song suitable for the group?* Think about the vocal range and the difficulty of the melody, lyrics and pronunciation. Children's vocal range develops as they mature. In the early years, it is likely to range from D above middle C up to B; in Key Stage 1 it will be around an octave from middle C to the C above. Most suitable melodies will move stepwise (notes next to each other) or include small leaps (notes in fairly close proximity). As children gain experience, suitable repertoire may become more chromatic and with bigger leaps, with more complex rhythms and harmony parts, switching between the head voice and the chest voice. The speed and difficulty of the words need to provide attainable challenge for the group. We can also expect more attention paid to expression and vocal techniques as children become more experienced singers.

- *Will the children enjoy singing this material?* This does not mean that all songs have to be jolly and uplifting, but they do need to appeal to your class, although often your attitude to the music and how you introduce it are important factors. If you are unfamiliar with the class or have not sung with them before, you might want to start with a familiar song. Repertoire needs to be age-appropriate. Be brave and try out things you may not be sure they will instantly love.

- *Does some repertoire introduce children to something new, and can you provide tangible links?* There are many idioms, styles, genres and traditions represented in music and these come from a wide range of historical periods and cultural contexts. Try to explore some new musical influences with children and help them to make sense of it in their own world.

- *Is the song culturally suitable?* The material should be checked to make sure it is suitable within each setting. In some schools, repertoire suggesting, for example, religious meaning may not be considered suitable, whereas in other schools it is fine and expected. This will be dependent on the context within which you are working.

- *Are the lyrics suitable?* You should avoid explicit lyrics or messages (direct or indirect) considered unsuitable for the class or age group. Language needs to be accessible to your class for them to make some sense of the words, and the words need to be within their technical capability when pronouncing them, which may also be impacted by the speed of the music.

- *Could you explain the lyrics if questioned?* This is particularly important in relation to songs with language that children may not be familiar with. You should be able to translate the meaning if in a foreign language or a language which children might not understand, such as words from old English or occasional tricky vocabulary.

- *Will it suit all of the voices?* At a younger age, our lung capacity and vocal systems are less developed (Sergeant and Welch, 2008). Additionally, we often think about boys' voices starting to mature as they reach adolescence and go to secondary school, making it 'somebody else's problem' in terms of primary school teaching. However, Martin Ashley's (2015) work shows that we need to be aware of boys' voices changing/developing across a longer period of time and from a younger age.

Finding repertoire

Online song banks including Sing Up, which was set up as the National Singing Programme, offer a wealth of material; many songs are presented as lyric sheets or backing tracks with and without the parts being sung, and also as slowed down versions of songs, which can also be incredibly useful. These are all searchable by Key Stage and also by topic. Singing is also central to the approaches to music teaching developed by educators such as Kodály and Dalcroze. There are many, many published songbooks which you may find useful. Some specialist organisations also offer resources. For example, the English Folk Dance and Song Society have a growing resource bank of freely available material linked to English folk traditions and many recorded and printed resources and ideas for developing classroom work at all Key Stages. These resources offer guidance about how to use the material for music education and through the curriculum in mainstream and special schools. The internet is a brilliant resource for finding recordings, karaoke versions and lyrics for millions of songs.

Teaching a song

Having chosen the warm-up or repertoire, you next need to think about how you will teach it. You may have a backing track or recording, or perhaps you will accompany it with a musical instrument. You may want to teach it unaccompanied, just using your voice. Here are a few things you might think about when teaching a song:

- *Knowing the song well.* Practise singing the song through at home before you introduce it in school. Try to learn the lyrics by heart – it is much easier and more natural to introduce a song if you know it well, and you are likely to feel much more confident.
- *Choosing a starting pitch.* Finding an appropriate starting note is crucial – the whole song should be within a suitable pitch range. The first note of the song is not necessarily the lowest or the highest in the entire song. If you have been given the note to start on (or once you have decided on a suitable starting pitch), play this on a musical instrument such as a chime bar and then hum through the melody to check that it all falls within a comfortable range. Remember that children generally have a higher pitched voice than adults – you could also ask the children to suggest the starting pitch if they are familiar with the song and adapt it if necessary.
- *Sharing the starting note with pupils.* You could play it on an instrument and then ask the class to listen to it and hum it back. Alternatively, if you are feeling more confident, you could hum the note and ask the children to match the pitch of your voice. Walk around and listen – if you have children who find pitch matching difficult, try to arrange the class so that they are near a confident and in-tune singer, or stand next to them yourself. It is crucial you don't let them know that this is the reason for the arrangement or you may completely destroy their confidence. Everyone can sing – it's just that some children take more time and need more encouragement than others.

- *Starting the song off.* Having agreed a starting note, there are various ways to start it off. The most obvious pre-starting sign is a breath in. It is good to get children to focus on you and breathe at the same time. They also need to know how fast to sing. You may wish to count in (and sing the number of beats on the starting pitch if you want to). Alternatively, you can clap or click the pulse with your fingers, or ask a pupil to do this. Note that children need to have the counting-in modelled and that the speed you count in (for example, 1-2-3-4) is the pulse you are setting. As children become more experienced, you could stand together and try to breathe together the beat before the song starts without counting it. This makes them focus more on the ensemble aspect of the experience.
- *Repetition is good!* To improve the sound and technique, repetition is important. This can be done in many ways, particularly by making it into a game (e.g. using a slightly different voice), so that children don't get bored repeating musical phrases over and over again. Playing lots of games going between a limited number of notes (e.g. G and E above middle C – the 'ding dong' sound of a doorbell) can help with securing tuning and pitch matching.
- *What kind of voice should you use?* Be yourself! Your voice does not have to be loud or in a forced style. Strong, quiet singing encourages focused listening. The important point is that it is your voice, a voice that the children know.
- *What about the lyrics?* If you are teaching by rote, you will be introducing the lyrics and melody at the same time. Overall, this is one of the most flexible ways to teach because it allows you to be reflexive in whether you move on to a new line or section, or spend a little time cementing the learning if it has not quite been grasped. If the song is long, or children are learning it from a recording, you might need to display the words on the board, but if you do this at the start, be aware that their attention will be drawn to the board and not to you!

How will the class be arranged whilst singing?

Ideally, they will stand together as an ensemble, either in a circle or bunched together. Sitting behind desks is far from ideal – it is much harder for them to feel 'part of something', there are many distractions and the spreading out of voices around the room has the potential for some children to feel self-conscious. Sitting on the floor for long periods of time is also not ideal.

There are various ways in which you could introduce or teach a song, depending on how confident you feel. Here are a few examples. In each of these examples, only the singing aspect is described, but you could easily incorporate movement to move to a pulse, opportunities to respond more freely to music, add actions, etc.

Sing along

Particularly in the early years and Key Stage 1, there is huge potential for singing your way through the day. Sing as children move from place to place, as you develop routines, starting and ending the school day, learning parts of the body, counting and reading stories. Children will start to spontaneously join in with the songs they know.

Put the radio on (choose your station carefully!) every now and then for 2 minutes before lunch and sing along with the class to whatever is on. Develop a list of class songs that you commonly know and sing along when getting changed for PE.

Teaching by call and echo

Sing a line or short section for the children to immediately repeat. If you point to you and then them as you sing, it makes it much more obvious when they should listen and when they should repeat. This is a great way to teach songs and warm-ups because it is done in small chunks and the lyrics and melody are worked on together and the musical experience tends to flow if you do not keep stopping to talk or explain. The quality often gets better by repetition too as it allows you to be reactive about whether to repeat a section or move on.

Teaching a small group first

If you are not feeling confident enough to sing to the whole class yet, you might consider teaching the song in advance (e.g. at break time) to a small group of pupils so that you can collectively teach it to the class. You might also have a colleague who is willing to sing with you whilst you teach the song. Observing other teachers may also give you more ideas about how other teachers introduce songs.

Continually singing through until learnt

If, for example, you are singing along with a backing track or recording, there is not quite the same opportunity for this iterative approach and it is more likely that you will repeat a whole section (or perhaps the whole song) until the melody and lyrics have been grasped well enough. It will get better through repeated singing from start to end, but it is very likely that children will pick up some parts both quicker and better than others, so you may still want to pick out sections to practise without the backing track.

Listening first

If the repertoire is not likely to be very familiar to the children, you might think about how to get them to listen to it first. This might be using an 'absorption' approach where the song is strategically playing in the classroom for a few days before (e.g. when coming in from break or changing for PE). Alternatively, the song itself might be part of the music lesson in another way and you might have an activity where children engage the song in the first instance through another means, for instance via active yet engaged listening (i.e. giving them something specific to focus on or do whilst listening that helps them to listen more attentively).

Internalising the beat

A fundamental musical skill is internalising the beat. You can play games with well-known repertoire using red and green traffic lights. The children should sing out loud when the lights are on green, and continue to sing 'in their heads' when the lights are on red, joining back in when the lights go green again.

Chapter summary

Singing is a fundamental part of an integrated and holistic music education in which children use voices and instruments to make and create music in a variety of ways and for a variety of purposes. It builds a sense of community. Singing in school could include children using their voices in many different ways and situations, experiencing and experimenting with, and developing, a wide variety of vocal styles and techniques. Our singing voices naturally develop alongside our unique speaking voice. Vocal work has huge potential to proliferate across the primary curriculum and also to extend beyond the formal boundaries of learning, into the wider school community. Unsurprisingly, research from the National Singing Programme (Welch et al., 2009) shows that the more children sing, the more they will progress musically, and there is also a positive relationship between singing experience and social confidence.

Getting the best out of children means making learning relevant and enjoyable. It is important to incorporate a wide variety of repertoire in which children's own musical tastes, preferences and ideas are included alongside new and unfamiliar music and musical experiences. We shouldn't under-estimate what children will enjoy singing and should therefore be brave in our choices of repertoire. Joining in with singing and anything you ask the children to do is critical. There has been a recent move towards whole-class ukulele teaching in many primary schools – what joy you can get from singing along and accompanying yourself! Then there is the kazoo, a simple instrument into which you hum or sing – another way of developing tuning and confidence. The possibilities are endless! I doubt you'll ever go on a coach trip with your class where the communal singing of campfire songs is not a central feature, so come on, join in and find your voice (but don't forget to listen to everyone else's too!). Find any opportunity you can to sing – in the classroom or out – and what about taking some singing lessons? Staff choirs are another brilliant way to have fun, learn repertoire and develop confidence and a sense of community. Children love to see and hear their teachers singing, whether on stage in a choir or rock band, on a video or in the classroom. Such engagement in the school community is crucial if we are to convince children that music really is for everyone. Having the confidence to sing is the most important action, without getting too het up about whether you are singing 'well' or 'singing the right notes'.

Further reading

Campbell, P.S. (2011) *Songs in their Heads: Music and its Meaning in Children's Lives*. New York: Oxford University Press.

Lamont, A., Daubney, A. and Spruce, G. (2012) Singing in primary schools: Case studies of good practice in whole class vocal tuition. *British Journal of Music Education*, 29(2): 251–68.

Laurence, F. (2011) Children's singing. In J. Potter (ed.) *The Cambridge Companion to Singing*. Cambridge: Cambridge University Press.

Resources

English Folk Dance and Song Society – www.efdss.org/efdss-education/resource-bank [has resources for teaching English folk songs, including scores, recordings, case studies and videos, showing ways to approach teaching]

National Teachers Choir – www.nationalteacherschoir.org.uk/ [a choir just for teachers that meets for a weekend each term]

Sing for Pleasure – www.singforpleasure.co.uk [publishes books of songs and provides courses for teachers]

Sing Up – www.singup.org [has a large song bank, termly magazines and lots of advice on how to embed singing with staff and children]

Virtual Piano – http://virtualpiano.net [a free interactive keyboard for use with a whiteboard]

Teaching 'methods' embedding singing

Dalcrose – www.dalcroze.org.uk

Kodály   – www.britishkodalyacademy.org

Voces8 – www.voces8.com/education

Voices Foundation – www.voices.org.uk

4

INSTRUMENTS, TECHNOLOGIES AND TOOLS

I'm awesome on the drum kit. I teach myself mostly and my Dad helps me sometimes but he can't play very much. I'm not very good at school work, Maths and stuff, but I've got loads of friends and sometimes at Christmas we all go out down to the old people's home with Mr Jones [music teacher]. We play and they sing. Some of them are really deaf but I think they enjoy it anyway. (Miranda, age 10)

Introduction

This chapter explores instruments and technologies commonly found in primary schools, offering ideas about how they might be used in your classroom.

As with the other chapters in this book, the subject matter does not fit into nice neat boxes. It follows the chapter on singing because vocalising and developing aural skills can greatly enhance our learning of musical instruments. There is a separate chapter on creativity/composing and improvising, so this chapter is purposely more focused on performing together. However, making and creating music almost seamlessly overlap. It is through the use of instruments, technologies and voices, either on their own or in any combination, that music comes to life.

Objectives

Through this chapter you will:

- consider different instruments and technologies used to make and create music
- explore ways to set up musical learning in the classroom
- investigate ways of using instruments through the music curriculum
- recognise ways to differentiate teaching and learning in order to challenge all pupils appropriately and to create inclusive environments.

Positive engagement

Children are usually excited to do music in school; the general babble that ensues when the music lesson is mentioned or starts should be taken as enthusiasm. In some cases, a teacher's lack of confidence in their ability to get the class quiet again and get pupils' attention can deter them from teaching music; the idea of not striving for a quiet and calm environment can be very stressful. In music lessons, sound is at the heart of the experience. Through employing appropriate strategies, children's energy and enthusiasm can be channelled into very successful music lessons in which expectations are part of a commonly agreed framework for self-discipline and participation through personal and collaborative engagement.

Getting children on side has a lot to do with the ethos and environment in the classroom and school. As obvious as it sounds, being positive and encouraging is key to this. Negativity is a significant mood hoover. Setting up learning so that all children feel included, their contributions are valued and they are able to achieve, is also crucial. Learning needs to be considered valuable and worthwhile from the perspective of both the children and the teacher. Key ingredients include the teacher's enthusiasm and energy, as well as their open-mindedness to all kinds of music and a willingness to be part of the musical community. The way learning is organised and accessed sends messages about its value and accessibility.

Many schools have policies and strategies for promoting positive behaviour and also for dealing out sanctions when deemed necessary. My general advice is to try to create a positive and upbeat (excuse the musical pun) atmosphere right from the start, where praise and reward are used frequently and consistently. The learning needs to be set up so that everyone feels safe to take part or to do things that they may initially consider risky, and sees that their contribution is both valued and valuable. Creating a positive ethos where children see you as a genuinely enthusiastic and approachable music leader, in an environment where the expectations for behaviour and commitment are clear and commonly accepted, is key.

TASK 4.1

Observe a music lesson and note all of the strategies used to promote a positive learning environment. Remember that some of these can be quite subtle, for example an encouraging smile, a frown or moving to stand next to a child who is chatting. Also, keep a tally of the balance between praise and sanction.

Establishing routines

Establishing routines is an important part of working with big groups. This includes routines for getting out the instruments, for getting attention back to you and for getting the class quiet without straining your own voice. You can use these routines at many points in the school day; they are not exclusive to music lessons. For example, rhythmic clapping patterns and 'copy me' games are parts of routines that you might choose to use in lesson transitions or at other points in the day for a change of mood, energy or pace.

Managing instruments

Possibly one of the most exciting parts of music lessons for children, and daunting prospects for some teachers, involves opportunities to play musical instruments. Some teachers shy away from this, finding excuses for children not to play instruments. In reality, they are probably worried about (a) the noise, and (b) the perceived lack of control in a normally quiet and orderly classroom. Both of these are justifiable worries, yet they need to be overcome if children are to get the most out of their music making. You should also remember that if you deny a child the experience of playing a musical instrument in your classroom, this may mean that their musical experience will remain forever impoverished, because you cannot guarantee that the opportunities will arise again at a later date.

One of the most important aspects of developing strong routines involves getting out and putting away musical instruments. This aspect of the lesson can be ordered and productive, or chaotic and leave behind upset children who didn't get the instrument they wanted, and a mess of instruments at the end of the lesson for the teacher to sort out.

There are various ways to do this, depending on the age of the children and the set-up for the particular activity. It may be that you put the instruments out yourself before or during the lesson – for example, so that they are just out of children's physical reach when sitting in a circle. Ultimately, the order you do things in depends on the focus of different parts of the lesson. If the first part of the lesson involves listening to music and responding without an instrument or singing, it is likely that having the instruments out will be an unwelcome distraction. In this case, you need to come up with a plan for getting them out efficiently during the lesson at the point when they are required.

Some specific things to consider here include the availability of instruments, for example whether there are enough for one each or a limited number. Will everyone play an instrument or will some do something else? Fairness is very important to children, so whatever you do needs to be transparent and acceptable to all, such as making sure that different children get an instrument each time and that there is not a monopoly on the most desirable instruments – for example, the biggest drum or anything that looks somehow different to the others (instruments are no different to swivel chairs as opposed to normal classroom chairs in this respect).

Using time productively

Teachers without experience of teaching music may find it difficult to tolerate children playing musical instruments when the rest of the class are still collecting theirs. There is sometimes an unrealistic expectation that children will sit in silence and just look at the instrument in front of them. Frankly, this is unlikely to happen. The desire to just try it out becomes overwhelming and they start to play. The teacher gets cross, the mood in the classroom becomes more onerous and the lesson starts to move in the wrong direction.

Given that, in my experience, classes of trainee teachers are also curious and explore musical instruments when getting them out, it is perhaps one of my 'top tips' that the teacher gives a 'task' to do whilst the instruments are being collected. This might be, for example, to find the most unusual sound you could play on the instrument; it might be more around deliberate practice, such as practising a specific rhythm on the instrument, or it might be much more free than this, allowing children to explore the instrument to find a sound for a particular character. There is not always a need to give direction to children – freedom is also desirable and certainly a big aspiration of music education if we are to encourage children to be creative.

The other thing you really need to do is to establish routines to get attention back to you in a noisy and productive music classroom.

TASK 4.2

It is the beginning of the school year and Mr Roland is leading the first music lesson with his new Year 2 class. He is keen to get them playing musical instruments as soon as possible but needs to set some expectations. Currently, the children are seated in a circle on the floor and the musical instruments are in plastic boxes in the middle of the circle just out of reach.

What could Mr Roland do to make sure that he will be able to get the class's attention back to him when he wants it?

Here's what Mr Roland actually did:

Mr Roland discussed with the class that it was his expectation that when he wanted everyone to stop, they would do so immediately, and that would mean that they would be good listeners and could get more music playing done. He gave the class 30 seconds 'buzz' time to generate some ideas in pairs about how to get attention back to him when the class were busy playing musical instruments and there was quite a lot of productive noise in the room. At the end of the 30 seconds, Mr Roland counted down 5-4-3-2-1, gradually getting quieter. Children shared their ideas and the merits of each were discussed. Ashok suggested putting hands in the air and shaking them around so that the class copied, but Heather pointed out that they wouldn't see Mr Roland's hands if they were looking at their instruments. Eleanor suggested playing a very loud musical instrument and the class putting their instruments down and their hands on their heads. This idea was liked and a cymbal was suggested. Then Michael came up with the idea that if the lights were switched off, it would look different and not just sound different. The children agreed that they could all stop playing immediately if the lights went off.

Mr Roland turned this into a game. Michael was in charge of turning the lights off. The children were encouraged to chatter about anything they wanted, but when the lights went off they should link their hands and put them on their heads in silence. The class practised, and when the lights went off almost everyone was immediately quiet, but Vivien and Ben carried on chatting longer than the others. Mr Roland asked what the class thought – Mary said it was nearly brilliant but that some of the boys had spoilt it. Mr Roland said they could have another practice and if everyone could manage it three times in a row, the class could have 5 minutes added to their 'Golden time' chart. Peer pressure and a bit of extrinsic motivation go a long way; this routine was devised, rehearsed and embedded for the rest of the year, and Year 3 got its golden time.

Ultimately, Michael's suggestion was similar to something Mr Roland would have come up with, but the ownership of the idea was given to the class. Additionally, the use of rewards valued by a class is usually highly successful, especially with younger children.

Storing instruments

Routines for putting instruments away will depend on the set-up in your school, how the instruments are stored, where they are going next, etc. However, it is important that you use the class to help you get instruments away and that they are properly assembled before they are returned (e.g. if the notes F and B on the xylophone have been removed to leave only the pentatonic scale notes of C,D,E G and A). You should be clear about what to do with instruments that come in two parts, for example a triangle comprises the triangle itself and the short metal striker, and these need to be secured together. Leaving enough time is important. As with getting instruments out, the instructions need to be clear and you may have a system where a small number of children are responsible for collecting up instruments of a certain type. The most important point is that your instructions are clear and that the children continue to treat the instruments respectfully and with care.

Clear instructions

The order in which you sequence instructions is crucially important, because certain instructions always distract attention. Often, these are 'you will be working in groups of three' (and they start grabbing the attention of friends), or 'you can choose an instrument' at which point their attention is diverted, and if this is given before explaining what they will be required to do you may have to start again! A good strategy is to write down the order for yourself so that you tell children what you want them to do and make sure they understand this (e.g. by asking one of them to explain to the class what is to be done and how long they have to do this) before giving the technical instructions about how they will be grouped and which instruments they will be using.

It is important that children understand the instructions and expectations before they set to work. A good way to do this is to randomly select a child (e.g. via names on lolly sticks so that it is fair) to repeat your instructions back to the class, or to ask another child to explain part of the instructions if they are stuck, so that they are not under too much pressure. Reiterate these if they are not clear – 30 seconds more at this point in the lesson saves significant time and confusion later on! Also make sure you give very clear time expectations, e.g. 'you have 5 minutes to try out some sounds and develop a repeating melodic pattern'. Young children work quite effectively and independently within a structure of short time intervals punctuated by attention on re-focusing exercises (e.g. sharing their idea or modelling a new suggestion), rather than longer periods of unstructured time.

What are musical instruments?

The use of the term 'instrument' should be liberally interpreted as we have endless amounts of 'things which make a sound' (and can be silent!) at our disposal to use within our own music making. When we think of the term instrument, we probably think of orchestral instruments, such as violins, clarinets, trumpets, bassoons, etc., or band instruments, like drum kits, electric guitars, keyboards, and then a special category which we might (unwittingly) think of as 'classroom instruments', for instance recorders, chime bars, tambourines, claves, boomwhackers. However, 'instruments' also include anything else that makes the sound we need – buckets, dustbins, wind chimes, radiators; even our bodies make a wide range of percussive sounds. Anna Meredith's piece 'Connect It' from the BBC's Ten Pieces is a very versatile piece to perform using body percussion – sounds made using our own body as the musical instrument (see resources section at the end of this chapter).

Sometimes children make their own musical instruments, for example using rice in a tennis ball tin to create a shaker, or stretched elastic bands on a tissue box. This can be very inspiring for children; however, think also about a cross-curricular link with Design and Technology – the actual making of the instrument is not really a musical endeavour and perhaps there is better use of the music lesson if we consider the purpose as being to advance children's musical learning in some way and find ways to use the new custom-built instruments to create and make music.

Instruments are not necessarily age-specific, although there are sometimes physical reasons that some instruments are, as yet, inaccessible to children of a certain age and physical development. For example, giving a 4-year-old a bassoon and expecting them to learn how to play it is a silly idea. However, as McPherson, Davidson and Faulkner (2012) point out, one of the things that draws children into being interested in music is the physical closeness to instruments and to people playing instruments. Seeing, hearing and touching instruments on a regular basis helps children to be inspired, to explore and also hopefully to be in close proximity of, and spell-bound by, live music.

A list of common percussion instruments found in pre-schools and primary schools is given in Table 4.1.

Table 4.1 Common percussion instruments found in primary school

Tuned percussion instruments	Non-tuned percussion instruments
Boomwhacker, chime bar, xylophone, glockenspiel, tuned hand bells	Set of claves, tambourine (with and without skin), tambour, guiro, triangle, drum (many kinds including tom tom, djembe and bongo), wood block, agogo, maracas, castanets, cowbell, jingle bells, assorted shakers (including egg shakers), drumsticks

---

TASK 4.3

Go through the list in Table 4.1 and look up examples of the instruments and find audio samples of any that you are unfamiliar with. If possible, also try to find the instrument itself and try out the different sounds it makes.

It is important to think about music prevalent in the local community and to try to include experiences which link to this. For example, there may be a thriving community brass band including a variety of different brass instruments, or the children may come across tabla (a pair of linked Indian drums), steel pans or djembe drumming. Wherever possible, you could think about offering these experiences to young people. Some schools have a wealth of 'popular' instruments such as keyboards, drums, cajón (it looks like a rectangular box that you sit on and it makes various percussive sounds), guitars and ukuleles. For a snoop around a classroom, take a look at the video clip of a primary classroom (Down's Junior School) listed in the resources section of this chapter. The clip shows the layout and choice of instruments and gives reasons for the thinking behind the choices made.

'Correct' ways to play instruments?

Most musical instruments have a range of 'correct' ways to hold them and to play them – this is not usually limited to just one way. For example, the left hand should be placed at the top of the recorder when playing it as a normal instrument. The reason that it matters to have the hands around the correct way on a recorder is that some notes, particularly those using the split holes at the bottom of the instrument, will be extremely difficult (if not impossible) to play if the hands are placed incorrectly. Likewise, it would be usual to cradle a ukulele with the right arm, strum with your right hand and change the notes on the frets/fingerboard with the left hand. Developing good techniques early on can really help in the longer term; bad habits such as playing a clarinet with cheeks puffed out is not good and will limit the progress and effectiveness, as well as affecting the quality of the sound, all of which can be very disappointing for a young musician.

Not being sure of how to hold and play an instrument can put some teachers off using them, in case they do something 'wrong'. The internet offers guidance on ways to play instruments and you will probably find a range of different solutions. However, musical instruments offer a wealth of possibilities for making sounds, all of which have a purpose, and it is great for children (and you!) to try these out. This also gets children away from thinking that there is only one way to play something and overly concentrating just on the technique.

TASK 4.4

Give each child a percussion instrument and tell them that they have 2 minutes to explore their instrument to find:

- the longest sound the instrument can play
- the shortest sound
- the quietest sound
- the most unusual sound.

Play games with the class to guess how a sound is made (listening with their eyes closed).
    Put children into groups of four and ask them to share their sounds with the others and then come up with a very short (30-second) piece of music in the group which makes the sounds into any kind of repeating pattern (ostinato).

Technology

Across our lives, we use a range of technologies for many different purposes. Engagement with technology seems to start ever-younger, with very young children being adept at using simple technologies on tablets and mobile phones, for example selecting music, karaoke, playing games and taking and viewing photographs. Mobile technologies are often integral to family life, with parents undertaking an increasing number of tasks via a small screen, regularly permeating the family's social space. Whilst on the face of it this might seem like a distraction from the personal relationships between a parent and child or between siblings, such technologies also offer possibilities for shared experiences and the sharing of music.

Within and beyond the classroom, technologies offer a wealth of possibilities. These are not a replacement for musical instruments, but instead add new sonic possibilities for making and creating music individually and collectively. A list of common technologies used for music with pre-school and primary-aged children is given in Table 4.2 (with grateful thanks to Duncan Mackrill for compiling this).

Tablets

Tablets are becoming commonplace in many primary classrooms and are extremely powerful and useful for teachers and pupils. Table 4.3 outlines the benefits of using tablets for developing musical learning and assessment (again with grateful thanks to Duncan Mackrill).

If you have tablets for use in your classroom, take a look at some of the amazing and powerful technologies available, many of which are free. A very versatile pre-loaded iOS app on technologies such as the iPhone and iPad is 'GarageBand' (Ashworth and Healey, 2015); it is likely that many children will already have used this outside of the classroom.

Table 4.2 A broad overview of the range of technologies available and indications of their potential uses in relation to musical learning in the primary classroom

Technology	Examples	Uses include
Electronic keyboards	Portable keyboards	Selecting from a wide range of instrumental sounds; use a chord and/or rhythmic backing; listen via headphones or out loud
MP3 music files	iPod or other MP3 player Online/'cloud' music libraries – YouTube, Spotify or Google Play	Playing songs or backing tracks from a physical MP3 player to support whole-class singing, rhythm or ensemble work Or accessing (via an internet connection) music from a comprehensive collection instantly
Recording devices	Tablet, mobile phone, portable digital video and/or audio recorder	Audio/video recording and playback of pupil work
Portable audio recording	Tascam DR or Roland R portable recorders	Making live stereo recordings in the classroom or in other locations
Video recording	Tablet, camcorder, Zoom, mobile phone	Videoing work in progress or final performances to build up a portfolio of pupil work; projecting on the board; sharing with pupils/parents via school network
Audio recording	Audacity (free), Wavelab	Recording sounds, editing (including pitch) and adding effects
ePortfolio	School or web-hosted Learning Platform, e.g. 2Build a profile, Edmodo	Pupils creating and accessing their own or a class portfolio, including audio and/or video of their work in music over time; and sharing these with parents/carers
Online music videos and 'how to' tutorials	YouTube, Ultimate Guitar	Teaching yourself using 'how to' tutorials and accessing a huge collection of online music videos, e.g. to support singing
For the more confident with music or technology:		
Tablet or smartphone	Tablets, e.g. iPad, Galaxy, Nexus, Xperia Most smartphones (iOS or Android); music apps, e.g. GarageBand, PocketBand, Nodebeat, Bebot, or virtual instruments and tools, such as Alchemy synth, metronome, guitar tuner	Arranging pre-created loops to make a backing track; creating beats or loops using drag and drop; improvising over simple loops or rhythms/chords; using easy-to-play virtual instruments or tools as teacher tools

Technology	Examples	Uses include
Loop-based sequencer	GarageBand, FL Studio, Acid, Music Maker	Auditioning and selecting ready-made loops from a pool (drag and drop) to build up a composition; ability (in some programs) to edit loops/instrumentation and record new tracks
Cloud-based software programs	Soundation, O-Generator	Online music programs for pupils to use both at home and school, to compose and create their own music
Live coding	Sonic Pi – software instrument for Raspberry Pi, Mac OS, Windows or Linux	Simple music-specific application for use in music to create loops and compositions easily, or for use in computing lessons
For experienced users:		
Sequencer	Cubase, Logic, Sonar, Studio One, Mixcraft	Making MIDI or audio backings as a teacher tool to support instrumental, rhythm or singing work in the classroom; using virtual instruments and effects to play back sounds
Score and notation software	Sibelius, Finale, MuseScore	Producing scores and parts with the ability to play these back

Table 4.3   Benefits of using tablets for musical learning and assessment

Concept/use	Possible uses
Provides a computer in our hand – sound, screen, microphone, etc. are all in one portable unit	Teachers or pupils can easily make video or audio recordings of completed work or their work in progress; this can then be replayed via a projector for the whole class, or on the tablet itself in a future lesson to remind pupils of their previous work (useful for on-going composition or performance activities)
	Key evidence of pupil work can be saved and collated and notes made on pupils 'on the hoof' in the class; this can also be saved to a pupil or class ePortfolio, replayed, shared and accessed at a later date
Portability	Allows easy internet access anywhere with a WiFi connection, so tablets can be used in different locations as a recording device or to support musicians as they work, e.g. in displaying lyrics, playing backings or simple loops to support improvising or performance work
Support tool for teachers	Enables teachers to play MP3 files, play backings, set quizzes, etc. and create their own loops or backings to support singing or instrumental work, e.g. using GarageBand (iOS) or PocketBand (Android)
	The tablet can be easily connected to a data projector to model, share work or present ideas to pupils

However, when using technology, we need to be mindful of the following important principle:

> It is not whether technology is used (or not) which makes the difference, but how well the technology is used to support teaching and learning. There is no doubt that technology engages and motivates young people. However this benefit is only an advantage for learning if the activity is effectively aligned with what is to be learned; it is therefore the pedagogy of the application of technology in the classroom which is important; the how rather than the what. (Higgins et al., 2012: 3)

The same could be said of any tool or instrument – it is not what you use that matters but how well it is utilised for a particular purpose.

TASK 4.5

Think about the set-up in your classroom and school and find a way to incorporate some kind of technology into musical learning.

Classroom layout

The ideal layout of the classroom will depend on the learning activities you have planned and the flexibility of the space. Many primary classrooms are set out with blocks of tables for groups of pupils to sit together. This may be suitable for some activities, where children are working together in groups (although the floor is often better), but, if possible, you should shift chairs and tables so that the physical space is better utilised.

Working in a circle on the floor

Particularly in Key Stage 1 and often in Key Stage 2, the whole class sitting or standing together in a circle on the floor, without chairs and tables, is a favourable layout. This works best when the teacher sits on the floor as part of the circle. If there are other adults in the room, for example teaching assistants, they should be encouraged to join in too. The layout helps focus children's attention and gets them musically involved. It directs the energy and attention into one space and creates the feeling of a 'community'. This arrangement is suitable for many things, including, for example, singing songs, suggesting and copying actions, playing musical games, sorting instruments into different types, having discussions, giving instructions and playing musical instruments.

Using the floor space

The floor space offers flexibility for children to be able to move, draw, paint, talk, play, sing, discuss and physically move around. It is possible to do many of these things whilst sitting on chairs behind desks but using the physical space flexibly and with a variety of spaces changes the learning dynamic. For playing percussion instruments, the floor is often the most natural way for young children to play without the table getting in the way.

Using other spaces

There are other physical spaces in a school that you may be able to use: the playground and other outdoor spaces such as the field are great for a number of purposes – exploring sounds in the outside environment, playing with different instruments (I have always found that children like to play with boomwhackers outside and often choreograph their own music too) and composing music in different physical places and ambient spaces. Taking children on a walk through the woods, encouraging them to make art and music from the natural surroundings, is always fun (for example, taking Andy Goldsworthy's environmental art as a stimulus for children to create their own natural artworks and then translating these into soundscapes). Some schools are lucky enough to have their own musical playgrounds – these are great to use with children of all ages. 'Going somewhere', whether it is to explore sounds, compose music or perform music, brings a nice dimension to musical experiences.

Facilitating group work

Numerous studies (e.g. Smith et al., 2005) note that children express a preference for working together. Most of the musical learning that you facilitate is likely to be in groups of different sizes and even as a whole class. As Beegle (2010: 220) notes: 'Musical collaboration provides opportunities for children to expand upon their individual musical potential through verbal and non-verbal social interaction.'

In the same research described above, Beegle noted that children took on one of three different roles when working in groups:

- leaders – those who listen, court and craft ideas from others
- social loafers – those who do not take an active part in the group's decision making and think they 'have no good ideas'; they are happy following the instructions of others
- dominators – strong personalities who don't listen to others and can ruin collaboration.

Being aware of the personalities, capabilities and strengths of the children you work with is an advantage, regardless of the subject you are teaching. Giving children roles and guidance, and helping them to learn to work in groups is extremely beneficial, and in the longer term it makes them more autonomous. There is often an unrealistic expectation that children automatically know how to work well in small groups; in a classroom there are often children who don't like working in groups, who do not want to work with the children they are put with or who are not wholeheartedly accepted by a group.

Physical space can be a limiting factor as children are often creating music in a group at close proximity with others. On the one hand, it is astonishing how many children are able to effectively shut out the noise of others around them and still concentrate in their own 'sonic bubble', but, on the other hand, there are other children (and adults) who find this unworkable. Strategies to help children to be involved include using corridor space and negotiating that everyone should practise at a quiet volume to reduce the general noise level in the classroom. More bespoke strategies may be required for some children, for example negotiating with them to stay for 5–10 minutes with them knowing that they can escape for a short period of respite to do something musically constructive, either with headphones on or in a different space before re-joining the group.

Fairness and equality

Fairness is extremely important to children and their view affects their willingness to contribute. Fairness is not just about who gets to play which musical instrument, although teachers should rotate instruments and give everyone a chance to try out different ones. Fairness is also about whether all children get a 'good deal' – is the learning tailored to meet their needs and expectations? Do children view the assessment of learning and the judgements made as fair? If they know they are being assessed, do they feel that the system of assessment recognises their developments, or is the assessment setting them up to fail?

Sadly, children's opportunities to take part in music are often unequal; this becomes particularly noticeable to children as they get older. Some children have additional music lessons paid for by parents. Some children go to musical theatre classes at the weekends, sing and play in bands and have access to musical instruments in their home environment. However, many others do not have these opportunities though they may wish they could. This natural inequality serves to heighten the importance of music in school. School provides a right to a music education for *all* children, not just those with opportunities, support and parents who can afford to pay. One of Paynter's (1982: xiii) guiding principles of music education is fundamentally about inclusion and equality cementing the importance of music within the curriculum: 'Music in the classroom is the core of school music activity; from there we can develop extra-curricular music making.'

Designing learning that builds on children's musical experiences from both within and beyond the classroom is another challenge which teachers need to carefully consider. Just as some children switch off if they feel that what they are asked to do is unattainable or unfair, others become disengaged if the learning does not build on and develop their skills and experiences. This also sometimes manifests as poor behaviour, and teachers should be aware of the impact of boredom on engagement and behaviour. It is good to encourage children to bring in their musical experiences (and often their instruments) and to provide appropriate challenge within the school music environment, including within lessons. This needs to be done in a considered and tactful way so that other children don't feel like 'non-musicians'.

Differentiation

Differentiation relates to particular adaptations aimed at meeting the needs, interests and aspirations of all pupils and offering appropriate challenge in all given musical situations. Often, aspects of differentiation are intuitive in that a teacher uses their 'radar' to alert them to a particular child or group's needs, achievements, focus, etc., throughout the lesson. The teacher intervenes as necessary based on their observations and judgement. This may be as simple as a word of encouragement or playing/singing along with a group to help keep them in time and scaffold learning through musically supporting them. At other times, children may be given a slightly different part or role to play, using different resources offering a range of different access points and challenges. The task or goal may be common for the whole class or may differ for certain groups. Some examples of differentiation in music are given in Table 4.4.

Nurturing individual needs

As with teaching and learning in any area of the curriculum, we have a responsibility to nurture individual needs. Music can be an extremely inclusive subject if set up well – recent excellent high-profile examples include the British Paraorchestra playing at the 2012 Olympic opening ceremony with Coldplay, and the inclusive orchestra 'o360' playing along with all the other young performers at a city-wide finale to the SoundCity concert in Brighton in 2016. High quality music and musical

Table 4.4 Examples of differentiation in music education

Type of differentiation	Example in music education
Task	The task set is adapted – in music this might involve rehearsing different parts of the same music which offer different levels of difficulty and challenge
Outcome	There is a common task but the outcome is different – this is commonly the case in music, particularly on more creative tasks
Content	Pupils are working on different content simultaneously – for example, some might be developing a backing track on computers, whilst others are using tuned percussion instruments to create ostinato patterns
Resource	Children are working on a similar task but have resources which offer different degrees of structure and detail in order to help them work out how to play a short melodic phrase (e.g. a short video tutorial of how to play the bass line, some possible note names written on notation, a pictorial view of the shape of the melody they are trying to work out by ear)
Support	Teachers often do this instinctively, e.g. playing along with a group of pupils who have difficulty maintaining the beat in a class ensemble, targeted questioning; not all support has to be offered by the teacher – pupils can support each other too

experiences emerge when substantive and targeted thought has gone into the planning, delivery and evaluation of teaching and learning. The bottom line is that in order to personalise learning we need to spend time getting to know the pupils we work with, identifying their strengths and unearthing what it is that hooks them into learning, in order to find ways to appropriately challenge them.

Example of inclusive music making

It was Friday afternoon and 35 pupils sat in a circle with a large drum in front of them. Tim, the school's deputy head, joined the circle and assumed the role of the Master Drummer. They 'warmed up', blowing gently on their hands and then making the 'sound of the wind' on the drums by swirling their fingers over the skin. Then the rain started and the pitter-patter sound of fingers on the drum skin increased as the rain got harder and then softer again. Over the course of the next 20 minutes, the group made music together, playing repetitive patterns together or as a call and response they had previously learnt which was linked to word phrases such as 'Ello, Ello, What's all this?' asked by the policeman, which changed to 'Bonjour, Bonjour, C'est que ce?', asked by the 'undercover policeman' and performed at a much quieter volume. Sometimes, when the patterns were in full flow, the Master Drummer, playing the djembe, improvised more complex rhythmic patterns which some pupils copied or adapted, whilst the others carried on with the known rhythms. Sometimes a pupil chose the next pattern, made a suggestion for a new pattern or directed the volume of the ensemble by standing or sitting in the middle of the circle and moving the 'magic fish' – a guiro – up and down. To stop the ensemble, the Master Drummer played with one hand and raised the other arm up in the air. Moving it from left to right, he said 'one, two, three, four, stop' (making a fist on the word stop) and almost every time the whole ensemble stopped simultaneously. Expectations were high and clearly understood and routines were well established. The joy of being involved in this music making was abundantly evident.

What we don't know from reading this is that every one of these pupils has a statement for special educational needs and that the school is for children with learning difficulties. Many of the children are non-verbal and most have limited language. Some also have physical disabilities and many have one-to-one assistance throughout their school lives. It is a highlight of the week at a special school in Brighton. I take my trainee teachers there every year; they are always blown away by the enthusiasm, commitment and quality of music making, and the approaches of the staff to facilitate engagement through careful support for children to play instruments without being 'forced'. Many of these young people also attend an inclusive community carnival band – 'Unified Rhythm' – pop along to any rehearsal or performance and you will be hard-pushed to work out which young people playing this often complex and challenging polyrhythmic music have learning difficulties. These examples very clearly demonstrate that we should have high expectations for all pupils; there is a body of research on 'expectancy effects' based on the work of Rosenthal and Jacobson (1963) and sometimes called the 'Pygmalion Effect'.

Unsurprisingly, this demonstrates that teachers' expectations of their pupils impact on the educational outcomes and children's own self-view of themselves as learners.

Setting up the learning: performing together

With instruments, voices and technologies, there are endless combinations of ways to make and create music individually or together. Regardless of the age of the children you are working with, it is often effective to incorporate instruments around a musical framework, such as a song or a piece of music already learnt. It is important that the repertoire or creative stimulus chosen is appropriate for what we want children to learn and to develop.

In the following early years example, the main learning objective is for children to accurately play the rhythm of the song:

> Twelve reception class children were seated on the floor with their teacher, Mrs Shepherd. A recording of the song 'Pease Pudding Hot' from the Amadeus Nursery CD had been playing at various points during the day as children arrived and left the room. They sang along with the recording and mimed the flute interludes, having been shown a real flute by their teacher (Mrs Shepherd had demonstrated how to get a sound out of it after asking the children for suggestions). Mrs Shepherd asked Luke to give a pair of claves to each child and the next time through, the children played the rhythm of the music on the claves as they sang, with varying degrees of accuracy but generally improving as the piece progressed to the second verse.

There are a considerable number of options to develop this work further – for example, changing the instruments, playing them louder or more quietly, one group playing the first phrase and the other playing the second before all finishing it off together, playing the beat instead of the rhythm, 'freestyling' with a different percussion instrument during the flute interlude and coming in with the claves again at the start of the verse, or playing the 'home note' on a chime bar as this piece is harmonically simple too. We need to be aware that there are many ways to fully exploit musical material; the main concern is that we are clear on the purpose of the learning and gear activities toward this.

TASK 4.6

Read the following example and note how the material was developed, the role of the adults and children and how the limited number of percussion instruments was used to good effect.

> Year 4 were gathered on the classroom carpet and were a few minutes into their weekly music lesson. Andi counted '1-2-3' out loud, grinning wildly and waving his arms around as he counted. A group of ten children, led by

Mrs Richardson, the learning support assistant, started singing 'Mr Rabbit' (from the book *Flying Around*); as they reached the end of the first phrase, Hu Ni, a pupil, brought in the next group to create a two-part round. The other nine children were sat in front of a glockenspiel or xylophone, sounding the notes C and G loudly on the first beat of every bar to create a drone. Mrs Tang, the teacher, kept the group in time by beating a rhythm on the tambour to slow the pace when it started speeding up. After twice through, the song came to a stop.

The song, which the children knew well, provided a framework for further exploration; children worked out parts of the melody by ear. Over the course of the next 20 minutes, the children created short rhythmic and melodic ostinato patterns (short repeating melodic phrases) on tuned and non-tuned percussion instruments and using their voices, drawing on words from the song such as 'ears are mighty long'.

Taking suggestions from pupils, a new structure was negotiated and written on the whiteboard:

- Introduction: non-tuned percussion instruments joining in one by one with their chosen rhythmic word phrase
- Unaccompanied section: whole-class singing twice through as a two-part round
- Instrumental 'break': pupils with tuned percussion mixed together their repeating patterns with a sonorous effect
- Unison singing section: once through
- Ending: a repeat of the final line three times, followed by an ascending glissando on the tuned percussion (with all of the tuned percussion instruments swiftly playing from the lowest to the highest note in one smooth slide).

Mrs Richardson video-recorded the performance on her tablet and the class watched back with great excitement, offering ideas for improvement. These were tried and rehearsed before a final performance took place.

Chapter summary

The most important thing for you, as the teacher, is to feel comfortable and confident to try out different instruments and technologies yourself and to encourage the use of them in your classroom. Setting up the learning in the classroom so that there are clear expectations and so that learning needs are met, helps to create a safe and productive environment for taking creative risks. We should remember that there is a range of 'end points' and that we should not always feel that we need to work towards big performances – and that perform*ing* is a process not an outcome – in the final example above, much of the learning came from the creation of the arrangement and the rehearsal, leading towards an informal performance.

Musical instruments have a magnetic attraction for children. They want to hear, see and play them. These hands-on opportunities are crucial to their musical development, and learning needs to be set up to allow them to feel successful and excited by making and creating music. Many aspects of musical learning are transferable from one situation to another, and development is enhanced through good quality practice, repetition and being critically aware of the sounds made as we play or rest.

There is significant overlap between playing someone else's music and creating our own. It is important to have a balance of these musical endeavours so that a wide variety of knowledge and skills are developed. Repetition helps to develop specific instrumental skills; teaching children how to practise is important. Choosing appropriate repertoire and developing techniques to get a lot out of one piece of music can produce some really well-developed and inspiring music, even if the material itself is very simple. Try to observe another colleague using instruments and then try them out in your own classroom – with a group rather than a whole class at first if you want to build your confidence. The chances are that you will enjoy it as much as the children.

Further reading

Ashworth, D. and Healey, P. (2015) *GarageBand for Schools: The Complete Teacher & Student Step-By-Step Video Guide to Creating a Song Using GarageBand for the iPad*. Book downloadable from: https://itunes.apple.com/gb/book/garageband-for-schools/id969094325?mt=13 [This online guide takes teachers through a series of tutorials and offers ideas about how to use GarageBand with children of different ages.]

Florian, L., Black-Hawkins, K. and Rouse, M. (2016) *Achievement and Inclusion in Schools*. Abingdon: Routledge. [This book gives practical advice about how inclusion and high levels of achievement can be positively combined in today's diverse school communities.]

Street, A. and Bance, L. (2006) *Voiceplay: 22 Songs for Young Children*. Oxford: Oxford University Press. [Built around 22 songs, this resource offers hands-on advice and concise notes relating to ways to develop voices and the use of instruments through musical games and activities.]

Resources

Amadeus Nursery – www.amadeusnursery.org/Amadeus_Nursery/Amadeus.html [this has wonderful arrangements of children's songs and nursery rhymes recorded on authentic (rather than computer-generated) instruments]

Charanga Musical School – http://charanga.com/site/musical-school/ [a subscription-based primary scheme for music education with flexible units of work and online resources]

'Connect It' by Anna Meredith from the BBC's Ten Pieces – www.bbc.co.uk/programmes/profiles/vyZCM3vdkYCWQk1GRN5sYc/anna-meredith

Down's Junior School music room – take a look around: www.youtube.com/watch?v=Lttc SpUmfUc

Incorporated Society of Musicians (ISM) – www.ism.org/blog/a-guide-to-key-stage-1-ipad-apps [has a list of useful apps and potential uses from a teacher in a special school, however the apps have great potential in mainstream pre-schools and primary schools too]

Musical Futures Just Play – www.musicalfutures.org/musical-futures-just-play [a skills-building approach for Year 4, 5 and 6 teachers through whole-class music making]

5

ENCOURAGING CHILDREN'S OWN MUSIC: COMPOSING, IMPROVISING AND DOODLING

What contribution can music make? It can give immense pleasure to the listener and the performer. This side of it should not be neglected. However, it is as a *creative* art that music is beginning to play an increasingly important role in education. Like all arts, music springs from a profound response to life itself … Perhaps we should place slightly more emphasis on creative music in schools than we have been doing. Music is a rich means of expression and we must not deny our children the chance to use it. (Paynter and Aston, 1970: 3)

Introduction

This chapter is about encouraging children to explore sounds and to make up their own music. We need not be bound by, or scared of, the formal terms of 'composing' and 'improvising'. Children need little encouragement to use their own and others' music and 'make it their own' – customising and bringing in their own interpretations, characters, ideas and adaptations, is the essence of these processes. The music children create themselves often includes elements related to music they know, and it is always interesting to note the diversity of the musical experiences they bring to their musical palette.

Many sections in each chapter are equally applicable more widely across music education (for example, encouraging shy pupils and encouraging creative risk taking). This chapter focuses on facilitating children's exploration and exploitation of sonic possibilities and the behaviours, habits and attitudes required for this. Whilst the examples are often linked to a particular year group or Key Stage, we must constantly be aware that musical development is experience-dependent, not age-dependent.

In current education policy, where teachers' performance management and pay are based on a defined set of measurable outcomes, practices unfortunately sometimes lead to children being 'drilled' in every subject so that they know how to answer test questions but not how to transfer their learning to other situations.

It must be very difficult for children not to be tempted to seek the one 'correct' answer or solution. A study by Hargreaves et al. (1990) demonstrates that children are adept at making their creative arts work proceed in a direction that they think will please a teacher. It is difficult to get away from this in education, but it is vitally important that we encourage creative thinking, creativity and originality.

There are possible tensions between wanting to encourage children to be creative, to explore musically and to develop self-expression, versus the perceived constraints of curriculum, of time and of a focus on 'assessable' or 'measurable' outcomes. We need to 'park' ideas about assessment and measurable outcomes and focus on what we think is possible, striving towards nurturing creative behaviours. As educators, perhaps we also lack self-belief that we can authentically lead on composing and improvising with our pupils, comparing what we think we could create with the amazing works of the artists and composers we admire. We need to get past this self-doubt, which is possibly based on our own limited experience, and find ways to become confident and willing to explore musically.

Most teachers (and parents) like the idea of encouraging children to be creative (it is probably on the list of values you created in Chapter 1). Yet, as Walker (1996: 79) notes, 'children are not encouraged to make up their own music; instead, they are always made to play someone else's, who always happens to be an adult'. This raises questions about the value and place of children's own music within primary education, and whilst this perspective is not recent, it is still valid. As Paynter and Aston's opening quote notes, we should encourage children's creativity and not deny children the chance for their creative music making to be squashed. It seems that, in some respects, little has changed since 1970.

Objectives

Through this chapter you will:

- develop your understanding of the characteristics of the music children create themselves at different developmental stages
- explore a variety of practical ways into creative musical exploration and your role as a facilitator
- consider factors that promote creative exploration and those that potentially hinder it.

Children's natural tendency to explore and manipulate sounds

As morning break began, Year 2 pupils Tegan, Eddie, Chris and Neala raced to the outdoor musical playground, proceeding to strike the instruments with great gusto. Moving from left to right, they followed each other along the brightly coloured bars, occasionally stopping to run a stick or a finger vertically up and down the xylophones mounted on the joints of the giant wooden structure and showing evident delight in the resulting glissandi and mish-mash of sounds. As Mr Street passed the musical apparatus on playground duty, Neala was standing in the middle of the group, pointing in turn to her 'orchestra', waving around her make-shift conductor's baton – a large twig. Her friends duly obliged, following her directions about whether to play or be silent, selecting sounds and carefully choosing how to play when their turn came. They took pleasure from exploring the obvious and perhaps less obvious sonic possibilities the instruments offered – scraping, tapping and striking them in a multitude of different ways and with different materials.

This example clearly demonstrates that children frequently make music of their own volition – exploring, adapting, selecting and combining sounds for their own purposes or perhaps with no fixed outcomes in mind; revelling in the joy of the sound itself in that moment. Such natural play, curiosity and imagination highlight the special qualities of children's musical creations; occurring naturally and frequently as children explore and engage with the world. It is highly desirable to bring this natural tendency for exploration into the classroom. We just need to work out how to facilitate it and realise that children do not need our permission as they explore naturally anyway.

Is the language itself a barrier?

Glover (2000) published pictures drawn by children aged 7–8 years in which a composer is depicted as a solitary adult sitting at a piano or conducting from a score. Perhaps these pictures indicate that children do not relate their spontaneous music making to composing. Given Glover's findings, we should consider the terminology employed when asking children to experiment with sounds. As a term, 'composing' sounds very formal; indeed, it is sometimes thought of as the process by which music is continually refined until it reaches its final form (Durrant and Welch, 1995) and, it seems, something done by very experienced adults to produce a masterpiece. Experimenting, improvising and playing with ideas get overlooked and may appear unrelated. In a child's world, many early endeavours come about through spontaneously improvising and experimenting with sounds, but the term improvising is also value bound. 'Improvising' in the music classroom sounds risky, creating worry that we may be 'doing something wrong'. Yet, there are no 'wrongs' and we need to constantly reiterate this message.

The language we use is crucial because the terms 'composer' and 'composing' appear detached from children's spontaneous music making. If the word composing sounds too serious, formal, elitist and unattainable, and the term improvising sounds too risky, it is useful to think about it as we would in art lessons. When invited to 'doodle', children enjoy picking up their implement of choice and visually exploring and creating. Doodling in sound, exploring an instrument, technology or group of sounds, is the equivalent in music. The way in which we couch ideas sends messages to children about what we are asking them to do. 'Fiddle around with sound', 'doodle', 'try out two ideas' and 'make up our own music' sound like easier, more accessible and achievable openings than 'composing' and 'improvising', and may remove stress from the task.

You, the composer!

Modelling creative behaviours, joining in and demonstrating your own willingness to take risks are all crucial. One potential stumbling block is that many adults lack self-belief as a 'composer', often due to their own limited experience. We need to get past this, and provide strategies and support for all adults in your classroom to overcome their own fear of trying, through exploring music themselves and messing around with sounds, instruments, lyrics, songs and voices. A great way to do this is to try things out in your own quiet space and be proud, and not ultra judgmental, of the music that emerges.

TASK 5. 1

Write down two lines of a known or made-up poem on a piece of paper. In a private space with nobody around, say the words out loud in different ways and voices and then sing them in three different ways, with any melodies that come into your head. If you are stuck, sing the first word on any note and then decide whether the pitch of the next note will go up, down or stay the same. Do it again, and this time try to experiment a little with the rhythm. Sing it in a different voice – for example, as an opera diva or with a very nasal sound.

Exploring expectations

Expectations are something we really need to consider carefully when thinking about how and what children are likely to create musically. When writing stories, they start with a blank page, not expecting to write a novel to rival Jane Austen or J.K. Rowling, or a play to compare with William Shakespeare. Their stories often relate in some way to things they have seen, experienced or imagined, and this is celebrated in the drafts produced. We offer them nuggets of help and suggestions and they go through a limited amount of redrafting sometimes, although as literacy teachers we are often happy that learning has come through ownership of the process.

Likewise in music, we do not expect them to produce something as sophisticated as Mozart, or as complete as a song by Oasis. What they produce is likely to bear some sonic relation to a smörgåsbord of music in their heads, drawing on things they know well or subconsciously, and enveloping these into 'their music'. To us, this probably won't sound totally original, particularly when they are very inexperienced in making up their own music in a classroom environment. Ultimately, we need to make sure that children are excited by making up their own music and that we provide opportunities and structures for them to try to assemble music for themselves, with a purpose in which they are invested. Celebrating their processes and outcomes is also important, even if what they produce sounds like an adaption of something or a combination of things they already know. As with writing stories, whilst we might think that a few iterations of redrafting might be desirable, in reality it is not always very likely. One reason for this is that, unlike a story, where text is written down in front of you, children often perform the music they have created and only have their memories (which are unreliable) to rely on, so a second performance is likely to be very different anyway. This is not an issue if you, and they, accept and celebrate the resultant music in the here and now, but capturing it as an audio or audio/video recording will help with future development.

Tensions related to children creating their own music

Children are adept at making up their own music outside of the formal classroom environment. Attention needs to be given to capitalising on their skills and motivation, validating such activities within the framework of a curriculum. There seems to be a 'tipping point' where the carefree spontaneity and freedom give way to reluctance and self-doubt. This highlights the importance of regular musical education from a young age; one which takes place in environments where everyone, including the teacher and other staff, is equally involved in the musical community and part of the trusting and safe environment where risk taking is the norm. The following few sections consider some of these tensions in more detail and through some classroom examples.

Purpose: What is the purpose? Why are the children creating music? Was it their choice to do so, or a specific task you set? Perhaps they have a pre-defined given or chosen task – for instance, create some music for a specific scene in a children's book; write lyrics for one verse of a song to which a folk song melody is given; find six different sounds on the instrument you have been given. Or they may simply be creating music for you to check they understand something you think is important; on the other hand, it could be completely their free choice.

In a free-flow reception class environment, children frequently add sound effects to puppets and characters, spontaneously make up short lyrical phrases as they move around, or play games and explore sounds on instruments that have been left in different spaces. This often happens by choice and not because someone told them to do this. The same activities may happen but may be teacher directed. It is interesting to consider whether children would go about things differently if they have not specifically chosen how and when to create music, and who to collaborate with.

TASK 5.2

Observe a child for a day. Note all the ways in which you see music as part of their world, and when you see them acting what you consider to be creatively. Invite a colleague in another age phase to do the same and compare notes.

Task 5.2 is always particularly enlightening with pre-school children because music, rhyme and singing are often embedded in the day; sometimes linked to routines and as children interact with others – other children, staff, teddies, dolls, farmyard animals, etc. Children often experiment with their voice when engaged in role-play; using their voice in this way is an important part of early creative exploration. They are naturally curious about sounds and how sounds can be made and changed using musical instruments and sounds in the environment. I always find it interesting to note how adults working in early years settings incorporate music much more, especially when they do not feel like another adult is watching.

However, as children enter the more 'formal' realms of education, there is often less emphasis on free flow and self-directed learning. Children probably still spontaneously make up their own music by choice outside the classroom, but most of their musical exploration within the classroom environment has a given purpose. It need not be this way if we carefully balance skill development and creativity in ways that nurture children's own music and exploration of sounds.

TASK 5.3

Can you think of a recent example where children have specifically brought something musical from 'outside' to school without being prompted? Here is an example:

Seven-year-old Katharine sidled up to the dinner lady and starting singing Adele's song *Hello*:

'Hello, it's me.

I was wondering if you would have a glass of squash for me?'

Ownership

If children choose when, where and how to make up their own music, it seems fine to assume that they see the relevance and purpose of this, if indeed there is a conscious purpose at all in the moment. They also have ownership of their music: they choose whom they share it with, whom to collaborate with and which influences and ideas they will use and adapt.

When directing children to make up music, we need to be mindful of the values we communicate through the tasks set and also through the ways in which we, as teachers, intervene in the process. A study of Key Stage 3 music teachers (Daubney, 2008) highlights that when pupils are engaged in a composing task set by the teacher, most teachers step in and offer specific suggestions for development, sometimes through verbal comments and also through musically demonstrating specific suggestions. Often, this appears to be linked to the finite amount of time allocated for task completion and also to the teacher having a set of 'success criteria' in their head. Arguably, this may stifle creativity and cast doubt on the ownership and worth of the music created from the children's perspective. It is difficult to ensure that ownership remains with the creators, but it is imperative to use modelling which does not suggest one 'correct' musical response (and instead models many possibilities), and to develop open and exploratory questioning strategies.

Focus on skills versus free exploration/creativity

I often hear teachers say that they want their pupils to 'be creative'. This is a great aspiration, and I was delighted that the word 'creativity' finally made it into the primary music curriculum in 2013, nearly 30 years after the introduction of the National Curriculum!

'Creativity', 'creative teaching', 'creative learning' and 'the creative process' are all terms banded about in education, often with little thought about what they look like in our classrooms or the relationships between them. How do we know that someone is deeply involved in the 'creative process', or that the resulting piece of work is 'very creative' and taught through 'creative teaching'? Linked to the notion of 'creativity' are the terms 'innovation', 'flair' and 'imagination', but what these might look like in children of primary school age is different to how we would see them in older children and adults, and, of course, they are very personal and situation-bound terms.

In arts subjects in particular, there is tension between the desire for children to be creative and 'free-thinking' and the need for them to develop specific skills and to deliberately practise. Both are important and it is likely that skill development may enhance creativity as children develop more technical ability available for use in creative ways. However, my experience of working with children has shown that sometimes those who are more technically adept (often through learning musical instruments in individual or small group lessons) become constrained by the boundaries of their self-imposed need to 'do it right', limiting their creativity and their willingness to 'have a go'.

In order to promote creativity in the music classroom, there are a number of aspects we might consider, including the learning environment. MacDonald and Miell (2000) demonstrate the importance of the social learning environment, noting that the ways in which we interact with others within and beyond the classroom, coupled with our formal and informal interactions with music, impact on how we understand and go about embedding creativity into our own work.

The types of tasks which are set also potentially either promote or stifle creativity. The promotion of creative thinking requires tasks that are perceived to be open in nature, encouraging scope for many different solutions. However, having no structure to a task might be too overwhelming for some pupils, who feel helpless if at least some of the ideas to get them started are missing and no potential lifelines are available.

Ways to promote creativity in the classroom

- Encouraging talking – if you observe a group of children making up a piece of music together, talk is always a significant part of the process. You could consider including a short amount of regular planning and reflection time in each session.
- Groupings – working in social groups in which children are already comfortable is helpful. This encourages risk taking as children are more likely to communicate effectively and easily, and already have a common understanding of how each other works. In a study of compositional processes with 10- and 11-year-olds carried out by MacDonald and Miell (2000), pairs of friends, as opposed to

children who did not know each other well, spent more time actually playing music, and outcomes of the resulting music were significantly higher, suggesting that transactive communication between children who know each other should be encouraged.

- Timings – allow an appropriate duration of time for children to play around with different ideas/solutions. We all come up with ideas at different rates. Make sure pupils know how long is available.
- Teacher intervention – intervene only when necessary and in a probing/inquisitive/questioning way, rather than telling or showing children what they should do and how to do it.
- Modelling – demonstrate a range of ideas and create a bank of 'go to' snippets of ideas for children to peruse as they wish, or not at all. These could be stimulus materials (use your imagination – there are many), short musical phrases or process ideas, e.g. 'Choose a note. Go up, down or stay the same. Then choose another note'.
- Purpose – make sure children have buy-in to the purpose and the process. Composing is unfortunately often introduced as a 'paint-by-numbers' exercise in which there are a limited number of options and the point of the exercise seems to be to show the teacher that pupils understand the building blocks of a particular style or genre by deconstructing a piece and then reconstructing it with a few of their own ideas thrown in (Daubney, 2008).
- Assessment – target setting, a process in which children can be involved in order to think about possible future directions and potential strategies, can be really useful. However, I would recommend that you completely avoid giving grades and marks and also stay away from the term assessment. Use comments, recordings and discussion to generate feedback and new ideas through an on-going formative supportive process. Having a rigid set of criteria by which pupils know their work is judged can deter creative responses, because it appears to become (and often is) a tick-box exercise.

Creative thinking

Creative thinking: (a) is the prerequisite for any creative process, output and outcome; (b) presupposes the active and intentional involvement of the person(s) who create(s); (c) can be fostered by appropriate education. Creative thinking is defined as the thinking that enables students to apply their imagination to generating ideas, questions and hypotheses, experimenting with alternatives, and to evaluating their own and their peers' ideas, final products and processes ... Everyone has creative thinking skills and ideas, but children have more because they are not yet fully aware of rigid logic and convergent views. They are divergent, open, inventive and playful, which are features of creativity ... Three factors contribute to be(com)ing creative: skills, environment (including means) and motivation. (Kampylis and Burki, 2014: 6)

A common misconception in music is that creativity is limited to the music children make up and not to other aspects of their musical behaviours or thoughts.

Great teachers weave creative thinking and action throughout musical learning processes and recognise that creativity can manifest itself anywhere.

Filling silent space

It can be extremely daunting for some children (and adults) to fill a blank space with sound. Creating plentiful opportunities to generate musical ideas in safe and enjoyable ways is critical, as is using a variety of different types of stimuli.

TASK 5.4

Consider the following scenario and decide how else you could help children generate ideas to 'fill the silence'.

As a little game at a transition point in a Year 5 lesson between geography and the final session of the morning, Miss Charlett gives each table of pupils a very short stimulus and instructs them to develop it in 3 minutes. The sounds given are:

- knocking knuckles on the table three times
- the sound 'Oh', vocalised in the fall and rise of a child showing their disappointment
- scratching fingernails on the desk
- a long 'beeeeep' at a fixed pitch which sounds like a microwave stopping
- the 'swishing' sound of the wind made by half-whistling and blowing.

Paul, Greg, Marcia and Alan work together on developing the long 'beep' sound. After repeating it a few times, they get into a discussion about what they could do – trying it out at different pitches in between the discussion, some higher and some lower, and adapting the length. Greg suggests layering it up so that one person starts and then one by one they join in with a sound and then drop out again, creating a natural crescendo, then fading away at the end. Through the short rehearsal, each child adapts the initial sound in ways that they choose, often spontaneously incorporating hand movements at times when they are 'beeping'. As the 3 minutes end, Miss Charlett switches off the lights and the sound in the room quickly subsides.

Valuing children's work

It is important to find ways to value children's work. It is not practical (or desirable) for each group to perform one group at a time, whilst the rest of the class is the audience. At times, this may be a model you want to consider, but you need to work out what everyone gains from the experience. In the example of Task 5.4, given the informal nature of the work and to capitalise on the momentum in the room, you might want to consider putting two groups together and asking them to join up their ideas – in other words, making a musical snowball.

Sharing children's work in some way validates the value of the experience. There is probably little less motivating than working really hard on something, the teacher running out of time and the lesson concluding without recognising children's processes and progress, and not having shared it at all with anyone else.

Shy children

Many children are shy at times. Sometimes this affects a child's confidence to join in, to speak out loud or to participate fully in certain activities. We need to encourage shy children to join in, yet be mindful that this needs to be done skilfully and tactfully and without making them feel under pressure. Specific ways in which teachers can help shy pupils include:

- setting individual targets and small, achievable steps
- quietly praising children for joining in
- using puppets, masks or soft toys for children to give responses through
- pairing a shy child with a chosen friend
- using a 'pair and share' strategy so that all 'voices' can contribute to class discussions
- not singling out any child to 'play' or 'perform' to the class unless they volunteer to do so
- making sure, during independent/small group practical work, that there is ample 'productive noise' in the room so that shy children will have a go without feeling that they can be heard.

Building an environment of mutual trust and respect between everyone in the classroom helps children feel confident to join in and contribute.

Musical starting points

Literally anything can be a musical starting point. Children bring wide-ranging experiences, influences and skills to their music, and also other children and adults in their ever-changing world guide them in different ways. Using our observational skills, we can guide and nurture children's development; only noticing whether or not a child can 'do something' when it is related to a task set may mean that we actually miss what a child does even better when it is not task related. Visual imagery, colours, shapes, words, sounds, moods, characters – there are so many possible starting points.

Experimentation and playfulness are key behaviours we encourage in children, so that they may adapt and play with different sounds, whether vocally, using instruments, using simple technologies or anything else they choose. We should value and support children's creation of music wherever it occurs; whether it is pre-school children bashing saucepans on the kitchen floor, experimenting with the sounds of different beaters on percussion instruments, making sounds of shapes from graphic notation, making up songs on car journeys that sound very much like adaptations of well-known songs, changing the words to Disney songs, trying out different voices and vocal tones for characters in role-play, making up their own 3-note songs on a recorder or selecting drum loops to accompany their own rap lyrics. The possibilities are literally endless.

Musical building blocks

The building blocks of music are combinations of patterns, pulse, rhythm, melody, harmony, timbre, tone, texture, speed, dynamics and the graduation of all of these. These are often termed the 'inter-related dimensions' or 'elements' of music. The danger with a list such as this is the tendency for these terms to be repeatedly artificially separated and also treated as absolute. Music is built around a number of tonal and rhythmic patterns (Gordon, 1977). As children become more familiar with the patterns through hearing and exploring them musically, more possibilities open up within their own music. From a young age, children 'feel' for themselves the musical changes through hearing and exploring them musically. It is highly desirable to continually offer rich and diverse musical experiences to all children to help them develop their internal sound bank.

What develops over time?

Perhaps the most noticeable development of children's own music relates to the complexity (structurally, melodically, rhythmically and harmonically) of the music, the coherence of the musical ideas and how these, in some ways, become more conformist, yet also more sophisticated, creative and experimental in relation to the organisation of musical ideas and material. Additionally, self-critiquing and iterative redevelopment of musical ideas become more pronounced features over time, and children's technical/physical skills to manipulate sounds also become more developed, providing access to more 'tools' with which to experiment. It is very difficult to identify exactly what children's music sounds like at different ages and stages; progress is not linear. Some examples of children's music making at different educational stages follow below, but you should remember that the resultant music is experiential, rather than age-related.

Early years

Two-year old Jacqui sits on the floor making a range of vocal noises whilst moving her doll around in the air. Rebecca, the nursery teacher, joins Jacqui on the floor, and with the help of a small brown teddy, initiates a musical conversation with Jacqui's doll. The 'conversation' continues for over 2 minutes, with Jacqui and Rebecca exploring different aspects of their vocal capacity – varying the tone, pitch, quality and dynamics of a range of sounds and moving the doll and teddy around in different ways. The music has a definite feel of flowing conversation, as the sounds go backwards and forwards in turn between Jacqui and Rebecca, sometimes with elements of repetition, extension and truncation, and sometimes with new ideas being introduced. Eventually, the 'conversation' ends with Jacqui saying 'bye bye dolly Doris' and waving her doll – the only identifiable words spoken during the entire musical interlude.

Young children are naturally inventive; curiously exploring the world around them as they make, adapt and select sounds. The spontaneous nature of young children's exploration of sound can sometimes sound like a 'musical splurge' or a stream of consciousness, a bit like an artist dabbling with colours, images, shapes, etc. Yet, as children gather musical experiences, they begin to use what they know and adapt this, changing the words, extending patterns, adding movements, changing tones, voices, etc. Very early in a child's development, 'copying' leads to 'call and response' through events such as baby-babble conversations with other children and adults, and the linking of movements and sounds.

There are countless opportunities for children's own music making in early years settings, and the role of the adults includes providing the environment, the scaffolding and the possibilities for these to flourish (as in the example above). It is difficult and unnecessary to separate out skill development and creative exploration, and, as educators, we should nurture both. Encouragement is key, as are opportunities for the development of awareness and metacognition, which, with this age group, means explicitly pointing out what they have heard, drawing attention to children's music making, being playful and finding ways, through musical and verbal conversations and musical play, to help children to repeat, extend, adapt and consolidate their ideas.

TASK 5.5

Plan and try out a short musical activity for a small group of young children that involves the development of some specific musical skills, and that also provides opportunities for creative exploration. This could involve anything – instruments, voices, movement, new or known songs or melodies.

Infants: Key Stage 1

Year 1 pupils sat on the floor in a circle with a range of tuned and non-tuned percussion instruments in front of them. Earlier in the lesson they had learnt a song about weather, suggesting actions and vocal sounds for different weather conditions. Using a simple backing track, Mr Robinson led the class in singing through the 8-bar song and then the children tapped their hands gently on their shoulders for the next four bars. During the final bar of this section, the voice on the recording counted '1-2-3-sing', a cue for the children to join back in with the singing. Mr Robinson explained that instead of the four bars with hands on shoulders, the pupils would use the instruments to create 'musical weather' to accompany pictures he held up, and then sing in between these musical interludes. To offer an example, he held up a picture of rain and the children experimented with the sounds, with many making a rhythmic pitter-patter. Switching the card to wind, some swished the beaters back and forth along the colourful xylophones, copying and adapting each other's musical ideas. Over the next 10 minutes, pupils rehearse and record an original version of the weather song.

'Fill the musical gap' games are important for children to gain experience of knowing how long sections of music are and exploring structure, but they are also challenging. The example above provides a definite structure for improvising and an environment in which children can feel secure in taking risks and experimenting, yet it also has a stimulus and a purpose. Further, it is crucially important to give plentiful opportunities for discussion and to recognise that, at first, pupils may produce an exact copy of a stimulus. Such activities help children to recognise and value the process, and to generate, bash around, explore and develop musical ideas. Dialogue is crucial; without this narrative, we do not know the ideas and thoughts behind any work, and can only base our own judgements and perceptions on what we hear, which is perhaps missing the point.

Lower Key Stage 2

As children become more technically skilled at playing a range of musical instruments and at singing, they develop greater control of the sounds. This opens up a wider range of possible avenues of exploration through which they may bring their own music to life. Moving through Key Stage 2, their composing and improvising are often more organised and structured, particularly as they begin to select, adapt and refine material more, although they are often adapting music they know or ideas they see and hear. There is often more 'talk' related to the generation and development of ideas, and giving a few minutes of 'planning time' pays dividends. There are many ways to introduce simple music technologies if this has not happened previously.

An example of using what might be considered 'traditional' instruments, in a whole-class instrumental setting, is given below. This is to purposely highlight the point that there is a great deal of room for improvising and composing in all music education settings:

Major Tim Peake's mission to the International Space Station has fuelled Year 4's interest in space travel. Recently, they planted 'space' seeds next to 'earth' seeds to compare the growth. They have been exploring music from Holst's *The Planets* suite, particularly 'Mars, the Bringer of War' from the BBC's Ten Pieces, and using the opening rhythm as a stimulus for practising different notes and trying out different combinations of harmonies – those which sound 'nice' and those which clash. As part of a whole-class instrumental programme, all pupils have been learning either the trumpet or the clarinet for 12 weeks. In this part of the lesson, they are encouraged to use these instruments to develop their own pieces in small groups based around the opening rhythm of 'Mars', with instructions that the piece must last no more than 30 seconds and that it must have a definite ending which is obvious to the audience. All of the groups' musical offerings are recorded one after another and played in assembly as the other children walk in, accompanied by a slideshow showing pictures from space.

Upper Key Stage 2

Through regular music education, children continually develop ever-wider experiences of listening to, playing and composing music, becoming more technically proficient at a range of instruments and with music technologies. The music they perform is likely to become more sophisticated; embodying knowledge of rhythm, melody and harmony, and giving them a wider range of tools and musical experiences to draw on in their own creative explorations with music. All of these 'developments' are likely to be reflected in the structure and complexity of their own music.

Schools and teachers can provide many opportunities for sharing and celebrating children's music both within and beyond the curriculum. For example, some primary schools have a Battle of the Bands evening, and other chances to share songs that children write for various occasions and clubs, all of which encourages creative exploration. Even activities that may, on the face of it, seem to be about 'recreating' music, such as the school band, choir or djembe group, offer plentiful opportunities for children to experience a mix of music composed by others and ways for them to be creatively involved as composers and improvisers:

> Year 6 is experimenting with a simple looping programme, learning how to import, audition, select and alter rhythmic and melodic loops. From a choice of four films lasting 30–45 seconds each, pupils are set the challenge of using their loops to create a soundtrack to accompany the film using the loops. Some of the children in the class are already adept at using this kind of software and are paired up purposely so that those with more experience can help others in the class to develop their technological skills.

As the above example shows, teachers do not always have to be the 'expert' in the classroom. There are many situations where children will fulfil this position and, as teachers, we should embrace this.

Chapter summary

> Music is a creative art. All musical activity – listening, making and interpreting – requires creative thought; the exercise of imagination influenced by personal choice and preference. (Paynter, 1982: xiii)

For young children, making up their own music is natural as they go about their everyday activity. Many of the songs and pieces learnt together in school or those that they know already form the basis of the music that children create. Adaptations and changes offer endless possibilities for new arrangements and new works, but we must make sure that children know that they do not need 'permission' to be playful with sounds. As musicians, and particularly as composers, we make creative choices; we should encourage children to explore the creative possibilities they want to. Nurturing creative skills in a supportive and liberating environment will hopefully provide the motivation for children to flourish as creative thinkers and flexible musicians. We need to offer these opportunities frequently if we want creative habits, behaviours and attitudes to permeate our classrooms. Literally anything can be a stimulus for creative music making.

Composing and improvising offer great scope for collaborative and personal creative exploration, yet can also feel challenging for teachers. Children's made-up music is frequently broadly based on or similar to familiar music from their own experiences, therefore constantly offering new rich and diverse musical influences is important. The music they base their own ideas on offers us insights into the music families listen to at home!

It matters greatly that you, their teacher, are willing to try things out yourself and model creative behaviours to the children and adults around you. We need to validate children's experiences, showing them that doodling with sounds is as much fun and creatively profitable as doodling with colours and visual ideas. Additionally, we need to remember that we perform and make up music for it to be heard, not as a theoretical exercise. Valuing what each of us wants to say should be the starting point, as finding our own voice is critically important. Creative work needs to be brought to life, celebrated and shared.

Further reading

Craft, A. (2001) An analysis of research and literature on creativity in education. QCA. Online at: www.creativetallis.com/uploads/2/2/8/7/2287089/creativity_in_education_report.pdf

Glover, J. (2000) *Children Composing 4–14*. London: RoutledgeFalmer.

Mills, J. and Paynter, J. (eds) (2008) *Thinking and Making: Selections from the Writings of John Paynter on Music Education*. Oxford: Oxford University Press.

Resources

BBC Ten Pieces – www.bbc.co.uk/programmes/articles/3xWSYQhHfM9dZYfmRmTwVqN/teaching-resources-for-educators-working-with-7-11-year-olds

'Listen, Imagine, Compose' from Sound and Music –www.soundandmusic.org/projects/opportunity-listen-imagine-compose

List of music education hubs in England – www.ism.org/music-hubs

Sounds of Intent Early Years Framework – http://eysoi.org

6
EXPLORING NOTATIONS

We make a lot of assumptions about music. We may need to get rid of these before we begin. For example, music isn't crotchets and quavers. It's not dots on paper. It is *sounds*. (Paynter, 1972, in Mills and Paynter, 2008: 26)

Introduction

One of the most common things I hear is 'I can't read music so I can't teach music'. As Stakelum and Baker (2013: 138) note:

> [T]he connotation that primary music can only be taught by the 'musically literate', someone fluent in standard Western notation, is rather problematic. The economic reality is that, in many primary schools today, music needs to be taught by staff members without such experience and knowledge.

However, Stakelum and Baker also note that nearly 40% of 79 in-service primary teachers in their study reported that they could read 'a commonly used system of Western notation' (p. 141), indicating that the reading of a notation system is perhaps more widespread than one might think. Clearly, the link between notation and musical learning is strongly correlated in the minds of many people. However, many musicians, even those who have had illustrious careers in music, cannot and do not need to read music. It is certainly the case that we can engage with music without worrying about our notational skills.

A fixed view of the apparent importance of notation extends to the views of pupils too. Campbell et al.'s (2007: 226) study noted a teenager's views of the importance of music reading and its role in musical learning: without music study, 'you can't sing because you don't know what notes they are or how to reach them' and 'you can't play an instrument because you can't read music'.

Given that notations are such a small (and often non-existent) aspect of music, it might seem excessive to have a whole chapter in this book dedicated to them. Yet, knowing that a lack of experience or understanding of notation deters teachers from feeling like they can teach music, it is very important to tackle some of the issues head on.

Objectives

Through this chapter you will:

- explore the breadth of the term 'notation' and how it relates to multiple systems and not just 'standard Western notation'
- consider the relationship between sounds and symbols
- gain confidence in relation to the use of notations
- examine potential uses of notations in musical learning.

This chapter presents some strategies and advice for using notation as part of an integrated approach to musical learning, through which notations are used only when necessary and helpful.

What is notation?

It is very interesting that many clichéd views of notation relate to what we might term 'standard Western notation' (also called 'staff notation'), i.e. a five-line stave filled with crotchets, quavers and clefs, etc. Yet, there is much more to notation than this. Notations can be any kind of visual representation – think about written music as a 'map' providing instructions about the composer's intentions. For example, the map could be a list of the order of the sections of music, coloured lego bricks to show the structure, coins, coloured counters and string to show the shape, invented notations on small bits of paper, a simple graphic representation of pre-recorded loops on a computer programme – all of these are notations, just as chord symbols, tablature (tab) and the standard Western notations are.

Notation is defined within the *Encyclopaedia Britannica* (Bent, 2016, online) as: '[a] visual record of heard or imagined musical sound, or a set of visual instructions for performance of music.'

This straightforward description notes the two important functions of musical notation and therefore alludes to the two skills needed to use it effectively. *Decoding* is the ability to use a 'set of visual instructions' in order to bring these instructions to life through sound. *Encoding* is the opposite process – creating a record of heard or imagined musical sound for sharing with others for the purpose of performance or preservation. However, these do not need to relate exclusively to standard Western notation:

> In the early stages, teachers may use a three dimensional object or objects to represent a sound or pattern of sounds. This can lead to the use of graphic notation, in which elements such as exact pitch may not be precisely identified ... through such improvisation and discovery, pupils can come to recognise the need to notate the music they are making, and attempt to meet that need. (Stephens et al., 1995: 37)

Within the National Curriculum for Music (DfE, 2013), the only specific mention of notation is related to Key Stage 2, where 'pupils should be taught to ... use and understand staff and other musical notations'.

However, this is not to say that notation is not useful or necessary with younger children. As Stephens et al. (1995) note, helping children to experiment with and begin to recognise the relationships between sounds and symbols is important and can be developed throughout Key Stage 1. The point is that notation *supports* musical learning and could be employed *when useful*, not as the central purpose within a unit of work or lesson or as a detached activity with no relevance to sound or a specific musical purpose.

Sounds, silences and symbols

Think about the use of notation in the following example. The musical learning sought is to help children to 'experiment with their voices in order to create suitable sounds for different characters'. Along the way, they will also be using notation to 'recognise that there is a link between symbols and sounds':

> Miss Martin is sat in a big chair with the Year 1 class gathered around her, reading out the story of *Goldilocks and the Three Bears* and sharing pictures from the large book. As each of the characters is introduced, the children choose a sound to accompany the character. For each of the bears, many children produce a progressively louder and deeper phrase vocal noises moving from Baby Bear, onto Mummy Bear and then Daddy Bear. The children join in with delight, adapting their voices and facial expressions. Some show the differences with their bodies. For example, David is hunched over with his arms wide when being Daddy Bear. At the end of the story, Miss Martin shows the images of the three bears in turn on the interactive whiteboard. She invites the children to demonstrate each of the three different sounds they have invented to the child next to them. As she shows each of these images in turn, the children perform their sound. She invites Justine up to the board to drag the images of the bears into her chosen order. The chosen order is:

> Justine retakes her seat and the class 'perform' this simple 'composition', changing the sounds of their voices as Miss Martin points to these from left to right. Once all six have been performed, Miss Martin grins at the class and carries on pointing to the images one by one in a random order. In between, she points to the blank box and the class remain quiet apart from occasional giggles and Caroline proclaiming 'there's nobody in that box'.

In this example, the children firstly use their own musical ideas to create the sounds of the characters. This requires no notation and is effectively following Odam's 'sound before symbol' (1995) advice. Following this, the children are introduced to the teacher's 'invented' notation, which is a natural extension of the activity, utilising sounds they have already and with obvious links to the characters in the story. The children recognise the relationship between the symbols and the sounds, decoding the 'musical score' and bringing the symbols to life through sound. Additionally, they recognise that music has 'silence' as well as 'sound', acting appropriately when the empty box is being 'played' as part of the music.

Activities such as this develop awareness of the relationship between sounds and symbols and an understanding that the symbols have a sonic purpose. Having recognised this basic relationship, it is necessary to help children be aware of how the nuances of music can be notated. For example, recognition of the duration of notes is an important aspect.

TASK 6.1

Try this example yourself.

Use your voice to perform the 'Morse Code' piece shown in the box below. Choose invented vocal sound such as 'Moo', 'Teee' or the ringing of a telephone sound using flutter tonguing. (All of these are more exciting than 'La'!)

———————————— •• ——— — — • ————————————

Such activities help children recognise the relative length of sounds and that sounds of different lengths are written down in different ways. It also establishes that music is read from left to right.

This kind of activity can be used in various ways. In the example below, two learning outcomes are sought, both of which seek to consolidate and embed recognition of the relationship between sounds and symbols:

1. To vocally experiment with the duration of sounds and recognise how the duration of a sound can be altered and symbolically represent a short invented phrase (encoding – converting sounds to symbols).
2. To be able to realise sounds of differing lengths from an invented score (decoding – converting symbols to sounds) with reasonable accuracy in the link between the symbols and sounds.

Year 3 has been learning about the invention of the telephone. The children have made their own simple 'telephones' with plastic cups and string, initiating conversations between one classroom and another via open windows opposite each other. Today, they are briefly working on their own to decide on the ringing pattern of their old-fashioned telephone. They are currently 'rehearsing' their ringing patterns, before noting them down on paper using invented notation. Earlier in the lesson, they played a vocal game following the conductor starting and stopping the sounds by moving their hand horizontally from left to right and snapping their middle finger and thumb together to stop sounds, making sounds of different durations.

William's invented notation looks as follows:

WWWWWWWWWWWW WWWWWWWWWWWW wwww wwww WWWWWWWWWWWW

Having 'notated' their telephone rings, pupils are paired up. William performs it by making a 'w' sound and running his index finger up and down over his lip. Michaela mimics the phrase and then looks at the 'written score' to decide whether it is an accurate representation of the music performed. Michaela says she heard two long rings, three short quiet rings and another long ring. A discussion about whether there is a short ring missing on the score ensues, following which William draws another 'short ring' on the score.

This short activity takes around 10 minutes, yet there is scope within it for developing knowledge of notation. Likewise, focused games around the ways that pitch (how high or low sounds are) can be represented visually can be very short but nevertheless impactful for helping children to note the relationship between shapes and pitch.

TASK 6.2

Perform the following using a tuned instrument or your voice:

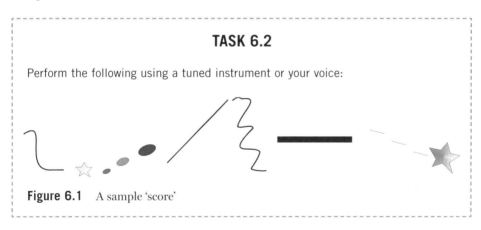

Figure 6.1   A sample 'score'

On the 'score' in Task 6.2, various musical dimensions are represented. For example:

1. The 'score' is read from left to right.
2. The pitch is represented, with higher sounds nearer the top of the 'score' and those with a lower pitch further down.
3. Music is made up of sounds of different lengths and silence.
4. There is some indication of how sounds should be played, e.g. continuously changing pitch in one direction or another (slurred) and those which are only on one pitch.
5. Differences in tone quality can be observed on the score.

TASK 6.3

Invent a musical game for helping children to develop their awareness of changes in pitch (how high and low notes are). Can you think of a form of notation that will support or enhance the learning?

Notation systems

When thinking about staff notation, there needs to be a clear rationale and musical purpose for its use. Additionally, there is much that goes before its use that will help with the learning of the system in meaningful contexts. As Turner (2008: 1) notes:

> 'In order for children to read and write musical notation with confidence and understanding they need years of aural/oral musical experiences that allow them to play with the sounds of music.'

Guidelines for music education, such as that developed by Zoltán Kodály and Emile Dalcroze, are based on the premise that children become absorbed in music through singing, chanting, listening, improvising and movement before notation is introduced. Being aurally aware of factors such as intervals (e.g. the pitch distance between notes such as G and E – the doorbell sound) is an important step towards recognising their relative pitch when both heard and written down.

Two aspects of standard Western notation systems are building blocks. Knowledge of these two aspects, representing the vertical (relative pitch) and the horizontal (relative duration of notes/the rhythm of the music), can be developed simultaneously as a precursor to the formal introduction of Western notation. Clearly, a musical 'score' can indicate more than this, but in the first instance the rhythm and pitch give an approximation of the desired sound. Whichever methods are chosen, developing the skills to use standard Western notation takes time. Like learning to read letters, words, phrases and sentences, we need to understand and 'feel' the multi-dimensional aspects of notation in a bid for musical fluency.

Arguably, by not encouraging children to be 'musically literate' we may be denying them opportunities to develop skills they may want or need to access some kinds of music, and are therefore placing a ceiling on their learning. The counter argument to this is that we need a balance so that children are not wedded to the musical score. A study of aural learning in a folk tradition (Daubney et al., 2014) found that some children who took instrument lessons were entrenched in a system which relied on the use of notation. They were competent decoders of the symbols and able to transfer these successfully to their musical instrument, yet lacked the cognitive awareness of the relationship between the sounds which in turn affected their ability to be able to play by ear. This also affected their motivation and self-belief because their self-determination in the position of learning a melody by listening and without the support of notation was diminished. This provides a strong argument that musical learning should be rich and varied, offering young people many ways in, which includes developing their cognitive recognition and understanding first, and supporting with notation where necessary. Swanwick (1999) urges musical fluency as the central goal of music education, relegating notational literacy to 'simply a means to an end with some music' (p. 56).

Notation systems are broader than standard Western notation. The system chosen needs to be fit for purpose and this may be dependent on the instrument being played. Figure 6.2 shows four chords to be played on the ukulele. This kind of notation is called tablature (or tab for short). It shows the name of the chord and gives a diagram showing where to put the fingers on the frets/strings of a ukulele.

Figure 6.2 shows the four strings on the ukekele running vertically. The line on the left depicts the strings nearest your face when you are playing; the line on the right is the string nearest the floor. The horizontal lines are the frets – the 'boxes' formed along the neck/fingerboard of the instrument. Your three middle fingers are numbered: the index finger is 1, the middle finger is 2 and the finger next to your little finger is 3.

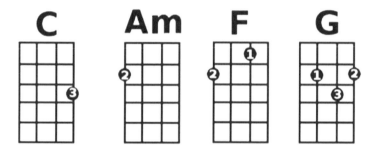

Figure 6.2 Examples of tab for the ukelele

The chord of C is formed by putting the third finger on the string nearest the ground in the third fret (box) from the left (i.e. the end furthest away from you and next to the tuning pegs). If your ukulele is in tune and you now strum, you should make the chord of C major.

Such charts are freely accessible on the internet and are a common way to learn music outside of the classroom, as this statement from a Year 6 pupil demonstrates:

> Sometimes when I listen to a song and I think 'Oh I like that', I might think that I'd want to learn it so I would go onto a website that gives you the lyrics, guitar, guitar like, tabs. I go on this one called Ultimate Guitar and it gives you the tabs for a song, so listening to it, really ... really that's it. (Daubney and Mackrill, 2012: n.p.)

In this example, the motivation to learn a self-chosen piece has led the young person to find what he wants for himself and to develop practical skills using a combination of listening and notation.

TASK 6.4

Try to play the four chords on a ukulele, as shown in Figure 6.2. Find an online tutorial to help if you get stuck.

Developing understanding of rhythmic notation

There are many ways to explore the duration of notes (sounds) and rests (silence) and what these look like in a written formal system. It is probably unhelpful to think about note lengths in a purely mathematical sense, i.e. to know 'how long' each note lasts without any point of reference. There is no defined order in which to introduce symbols, but often the symbols for the crotchet ♩ (1 beat) and quavers in pairs ♫ (half a beat each) – are introduced first through having had physical experiences of moving, singing and playing. An example of this includes games where rhythms for word patterns from songs are learnt, clapped back and then shown, such as:

'Waiting at the bus stop' ♫ ♫ ♩ ♩

'I love daffoldils' ♩ ♩ ♫ ♩

Figure 6.3 shows note values and the value of rests. These are all relative though, and such a table only gives 'knowledge about' music, not the 'knowledge how' that we are seeking in the first instance.

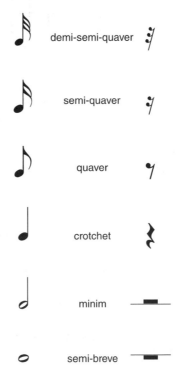

𝅘𝅥𝅳	demi-semi-quaver 𝄿
𝅘𝅥𝅯	semi-quaver 𝄿
♪	quaver 𝄾
♩	crotchet 𝄾
𝅗𝅥	minim —
𝅝	semi-breve —

Figure 6.3   Symbols for notes and rests of different lengths used in Standard Western notation

Figure 6.3 shows how the note lengths relate to each other, and how many are in four beats (which is often the 'length' of one bar). The names on the right-hand side relate to an American naming system, where a semibreve (worth four beats) is called a whole note, and so the other notes are named as fractions of this (e.g. four crotchets equal one semibreve so these are called quarter notes).

Perhaps one of the reasons that children (and adults) have a misguided view that being a 'musician' relates strongly to the ability to read music comes from approaches to instrumental teaching. It is unfortunately the case that in many early musical instrumental learning experiences progress is limited by, and linked to, a child's ability to decode music because some teachers teach in ways that are very wedded to 'notation first'. The relationship between the sounds is not fully explored aurally before the system of notation takes a priority seat in musical learning. Crucially, however, as Turner's earlier quote alludes to, we should: 'Train the ear before the eye – the ear should be familiar with the sounds of the notes before the symbol is introduced in notation' (Geoghegan, 2006).

In terms of early development, frequently playing rhythm games related to clapping, stamping, tapping and movement in general are advocated. Words and syllables help children to repeat rhythmic patterns more easily.

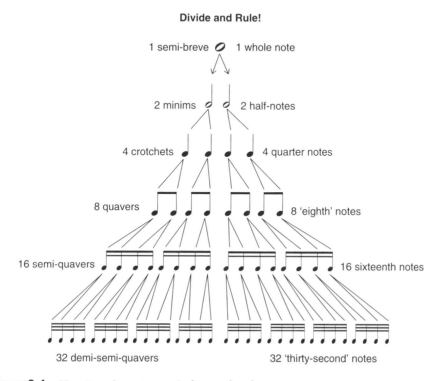

Figure 6.4 How to write notes equivalent to four beats

Note: with thanks to Roland Bryce for the graphic from his theory book

TASK 6.4

Read through the following examples of lessons and consider the following questions:

1. Is notation used to support/extend the musical learning or as the focus of the learning?

2. (How) does the lesson content relate to the idea of learning through game playing and getting sounds into the children's heads before notation is introduced?

3. Which is the more musically engaging lesson and why?

Example 1

The Year 2 class at Worlds End Red School is learning about the length of notes. Miss Mullins holds up flash cards of crotchets and quavers, explaining that each of the quavers is worth half that of a crotchet. She claps four crotchets and then eight quavers and shows what this looks like on flash cards. Miss Mullins splits the class into pairs, giving each pair a set of crotchet and quaver flash cards. Their task is to put these cards into a chosen order and clap the rhythms. They are given 3 minutes to try out different combinations of patterns. It is noticeable that the quavers are sometimes clapped unevenly as some children struggle with the task.

Example 2

At Worlds End Orange School, the Year 2 class has been learning a song called 'Who stole the cookie from the cupboard in the kitchen?' Mr Henry claps the rhythm of the words 'cupboard in the kitchen' and the class repeats it. He repeats this once more and the class echoes it.

He then claps the same rhythm ♫ ♫ ♩ ♩ and changes the language to 'ta-te ta-te ta ta'. The class repeats it and this whole phrase is repeated again, with Mr Henry tapping his knees instead of clapping his hands. He holds up the notation and says the phrase again whilst pointing to the symbols on the magnetic board. Mr Henry asks for a volunteer; Richard steps up and reorganises the order of the rhythm. Mr Henry counts to 4 and the class 'reads' the rhythm, chanting 'ta-te ta ta-te ta' as they clap the rhythm. More copies of the same magnetic symbols are produced and Sophie rearranges them again. The class reads and chants the longer rhythm. Mr Henry then ignores the notation and goes back to developing the quality of the singing and the rhythmic accuracy of the final part of the song. The lyric in the final line of the song is 'sent straight to bed by his very cross mum!'. The class repeats this line in different voices and Mr Henry claps the rhythm

♩ ♫ ♩ ♫ ♫ ♩ ♩ as it is sung. Mr Henry stops the singing and gives an envelope to groups of four pupils containing separate laminated cards with different phrases from the song and many cards of crotchets and quavers. He challenges the class to match the phase with the rhythmic notation, encouraging the children to sing it through in their heads and then out loud. After 2 minutes, the 'solutions' are left on the floor and the children rotate to other groups, trying out their rhythmic patterns.

Note: Example 2 uses a common rhythmic naming system which is adapted from the Kodály method.

Building understanding of pitch in standard Western notation

As previously discussed in this chapter and elsewhere, it is crucial that children are cognitively engaged with the music they make, create and listen to, in order to help them aurally recognise and 'feel' changes in pitch, as shown by their bodies in the following example:

> The Year 2 is sitting together on the floor playing the 'stairs and escalators game'. Jess has been appointed as the conductor. With her hands, she either shows the giant walking up or down the stairs (hands move up and down in small jumps) or riding up and down the escalator (hands sliding up or down). As she 'conducts' the class to follow her directions with their voices, four children use tuned percussion instruments, either carefully playing ascending or descending notes individually or sliding their beaters in response to Jess's instructions. Mrs Bedford holds Kevin's xylophone up at an angle so that it is obvious to him which way the pitch goes 'up' and which is 'down', as he initially moved his beater in the opposite direction to the musical flow.

> Mrs Bedford increases the level of challenge by asking half the class to continue what they are doing, whilst the rest, with their backs turned away from Jess, use their ears rather than their eyes to ascertain whether the music is moving up and down by step or as a smooth glissando (slide). Whilst there is always a very slight delay between those performing and those 'reacting', it is clear to Mrs Bedford that the majority of the children with their backs to the conductor understand the direction and speed of travel and where rests occur. The class swaps over and a new conductor is appointed.

In order to begin to move towards using pitch notation appropriately, there is a lot of 'knowledge how' required. There is also some 'knowledge about' – for example, that the musical alphabet only utilises seven letters: A, B, C, D, E, F and G, and there are 12 semitones in one octave. Most important to work out is how the sounds of different pitches relate to each other and the direction of travel. In the first instance, it is important that children have considerable experience of the sounds through making, creating and listening to music. Figure 6.5 is included as a 'reference' for you about where notes are located on the stave in relation to the treble clef.

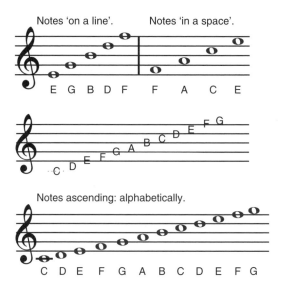

Figure 6.5   The placement of notes relative to the treble clef using staff notation

Some strategies for helping to develop pitch notation awareness

Crucially, children need plenty of opportunities to play with sounds and internalise sounds *before* being introduced to pitch notation. The following strategies are a few examples of the many that you may think about using, with a focus on playing games and using notation alongside a cognitive awareness of the relationships between sounds. You will find other ideas in many resource publications, including those developed to support the implementation of the National Curriculum for Music (ESAG, 2013).

1. Consider showing movement with the body, playing listening and copying games, asking children to work out the shape of a simple melody by ear that they have internalised by singing melodies with notes in close proximity (e.g. moving up a scale C, D and E using tuned percussion, or working out a musical cell with notes of an arpeggio or a chord such as G major – using the notes G, B and D) are all practical ways to help children engage cognitively with sounds.
2. Use a graphic notation game to recognise a melody that has been internalised through singing from a choice of three (of which two 'notated' melodies show the wrong shape).
3. Ask children to write down the short melody they have developed/composed/ improvised on tuned percussion, in order to share it with someone else in any way they wish (i.e. invented notation).
4. Think about the last three notes of a song they know well, such as *Three Blind Mice*, and ask them to sing this out loud, work out the shape and then lay out counters showing the shape.
5. Put extracts of notation on the whiteboard for the children to visually follow the shape when singing a song they know well; stop during a phrase and ask them to work out where on the notation the music has stopped.

6. Learn songs and play games on two notes (G and E) and then show these on two lines of stave; ask children to compose their own melodies using these notes. It is a great way to start bringing pitch and rhythm together.

7. Add in the note in the space between G and E and see if the children can 'guess' what this 'passing note' sounds like – it helps them to understand that lines and spaces are used when writing standard notation and to begin to explore the visual and the aural.

8. Learn simple melodies on instruments by ear (through singing them first) and then look at the notation to help children develop the relationship between what they play, hear, imagine and see.

9. Line up eight children, with the names C, D, E, F, G, A, B, C (from left to right). Check that the pupils know which letters are either side (in order to recognise the repeating patterns of the letter names).

10. Treat the lined-up children as if they were hand bells, playing and singing simple melodies which the pupils know well, then transferring this to looking at it on a stave.

11. Think about how you could use children's mark-making as musical score.

These suggestions include a substantial amount of important ideas – from taking internalised sounds and turning them into shapes and then, more formally, notes and specific symbols, through recognising the way in which notes sound and names are organised on the stave, using these to write and read music. The complexity of the skills needed in order to become a fluent encoder and decoder of notation means that their introduction needs to be carefully managed and that the notation does not get in the way of the musical engagement.

Chapter summary

There is much that all teachers can do to help children use notations meaningfully, whether or not the teachers are fluent users of standard notation systems. However, the ways in which notations are used also run the risk of isolating the symbols and making the notation pointless and confusing. As Odam (1995: 46–7) reminds us: 'teachers should never allow the task of writing notation to become divorced from the musical context. The need to write something down must be there, otherwise the motivation to learn will not arise.'

Teachers need to think about the musical context, deciding if and how notation might be used to support learning. Children invent some fantastic notations when they see the need to do so. However, we also need to be mindful that using it in the wrong way and at the wrong time might limit children's learning. As Kaschub and Smith (2009: 149) note: 'The confines of learning notation may impede creative thinking as children opt to set aside complex musical ideas that are simply too difficult for them to accurately notate.'

Chapter 5 discusses the potential issues with helping children to get the music *into* and *out of* their heads and to be able to realise it in some way. These issues may be compounded even further if notation is involved and, in this case, will get in the way of the possibilities of the musical learning journey.

These ideas are not new; as Fletcher Copp noted in 1916:

> The motive, then, for learning musical notation must be for the purpose of freeing the child by giving him the means of expressing his own ideas on paper as well as giving him pleasure in reading easily and joyfully the thoughts of others. The means used for the attainment of these ends are most important. They must cultivate as many of the child's senses as possible. If he can feel the symbols as well as see them; if he may see them in a big, tangible form; then through this touch contact and through this ready sight, it occurs to him to place the symbols thus and so and then to find out on the piano what the symbols so placed by himself will express when sounded.

However, the symbols in any system can be a confusing code to crack and it takes effort to get to a point of fluency. There are various levels of complexity to transferring sounds effectively on and off musical instruments and voices. Reading (decoding) the music and not thinking about what it sounds like can lead to extremely unmusical and unrecognisable renditions of known pieces, which can lead us to question the purpose of focusing learning music in this way and also whether the child in question understands enough about the coding system and the relationship to sounds in general and the instrument. After all, how can you expect fluency when a child is learning their way around a xylophone, looking at the note names on the instrument and looking up and down from a notated music example and prone to losing their place on the score every time they take their eye away? This case from Hubicki and Miles (1991: 63) exemplifies the point about the confusion of the system of symbols and their relationship with other aspects of sound production:

> we know of at least one beginner who, when shown black and white notes on the piano, immediately assumed that they would be represented by the black and white parts of the musical staff! There is the further difficulty that every black or white symbol represents both pitch and time.

We also need to remember that music is there in our everyday lives. We sing music, play music, listen to music, feel, make aesthetic judgements about music, are moved by music, physically move to music, all without the need for notation. We get it 'into' our heads through other ways apart from reading and decoding notation; musical engagement comes naturally through our ears first. Hopefully from this chapter you recognise that the lack of ability to fluently read and write standard Western notation is not a reason that someone cannot teach or learn music. Neither is it, in my view, a significant focus of a musical education nor particularly important to many aspects of musical learning, particularly during the primary years. We need to counteract the position that children start to sort themselves into musicians and non-musicians based on their perceptions of their ability to read music. If this happens in your class, it is time to investigate the sources of the values being adopted and find ways to adapt these accordingly. After all, as Swanwick (1999: 45) laments, 'if we get fixated by the notation, we may find ourselves barking at the print ... with little idea of meaning', which completely negates the purpose of using it in the first place.

Further reading

Barratt, M. (1997) A view of young children's musical thinking. *Research Studies in Music Education*, 8(1): 2–14.

Resources

Rhythm for Reading – http://rhythmforreading.com [whilst this is a 'reading intervention programme', it relates strongly to the reading of rhythms, as the name suggests, with the aim of improving reading skills and phonological awareness]

7

PLANNING MUSICAL LEARNING

'I love it when a plan comes together'
(John 'Hannibal' Smith: The A-Team)

Music educators internationally are united by a common purpose; to engage children and youth in music and to develop their artistic life and their humanity. To achieve that purpose they advocate the values of music, develop instructional programmes that are comprehensive and dynamic, and expand what is known about music teaching and learning through reflective practice and participation in research and inquiry. In these and other ways, music educators serve to build on past traditions and open the way to cultural transformation through the imaginative and creative contributions of a new generation of music makers. (McCarthy, 2012: 40)

Introduction

As McCarthy notes, part of our role is to plan and implement 'comprehensive and dynamic' musical learning opportunities for all children. It resonates with ideas contained within this book, particularly about our values being the philosophical underpinning of our curriculum and approaches. Planning becomes 'dynamic' when it is iterative – based on continual reflective and reflexive processes.

This chapter considers the integration of curriculum choices, pedagogies and assessment – foundation stones for promoting and nurturing musical learning in your classroom. Drawing on the content of the other chapters in the book, this chapter provides a framework for planning for children across their early years and primary education.

Objectives

Through this chapter you will:

- develop your understanding of the processes involved in effective planning for musical learning
- explore the integral relationship between curriculum, pedagogy and assessment and how these impact on the planning of teaching and learning
- consider how to plan a short activity, a full lesson and a unit of work
- integrate your existing knowledge into planning for musical learning.

TASK 7.1

These questions provide opportunities to think about what planning is and whom it is for:

1. What does the term 'planning' mean to you?
2. What planning (either in progress or already completed) have you seen in school that relates to musical learning? What time span does this planning cover (e.g. a lesson, a unit of work, a whole year or Key Stage; an instrumental/vocal teaching scheme for a term or a year)?
3. What are the potential advantages of planning? Are there any potential problems and barriers?
4. Who are you planning for?
5. What do you find are useful thinking prompts and titles for sections on a lesson plan when planning for musical learning? Write a list.

Defining planning

There are various different types of plans that you might come across or need to create in school. It is possible that your school has a 'roadmap' – a 'long-term plan' of musical learning across the school, which may be split down into Key Stages or years. Sometimes this is just a list of topics or stimulus material; more useful examples broadly outline learning goals. From this, *medium-term plans* can be constructed. These are usually units of work for a half term or term. In the better examples of medium-term planning, the curriculum and learning goals are well defined and it is clear how learning tasks in individual units consolidate and build on prior learning. *Short-term planning* usually relates to the plans for individual lessons, which help define the desired learning, how the lesson will guide learners towards desired learning, and other details such as how the teacher will decide on the relative success of the lesson, what materials are required, and notes about particular children which the teacher will need to be aware of and possibly plan differently for. Remember though, a plan is just that – a plan. There are a multitude of reasons why we might just throw it out of the window and either go with what we see unravelling in the classroom or off on a more suitable tangent for that moment.

Schools or training providers probably provide their own pro-forma to complete in advance of lessons and to frame post-lesson reflection. You should think of lesson plans and unit plans as a flexible 'thinking framework' to help you create learning experiences that help all children to achieve and to make progress, no matter what their starting point.

Classes and schools are all different. Great planning is that which creates learning experiences especially for children in the class or group. The National Curriculum (DfE, 2013) is extremely detailed for some subjects; for instance, Mathematics is 47 pages long and expectations for what pupils will be taught in every school year are broken down in detail. Happily, the National Curriculum for Music is much more flexible, which provides opportunities to take the musical learning in a direction you decide and which you consider to be desirable for the children you are working with. This means that the musical learning and curriculum in your school may look very different to that in other local schools.

Planning for musical learning

Planning for musical learning should begin with an understanding of where pupils are in their learning journey. As defined and explored through the previous chapters in this book, musical learning is built around six main strands of learning:

- singing
- composing
- improvising
- playing
- critical engagement
- spiritual, moral, social and culture (SMSC).

Listening is not listed separately as it is absolutely integral to making and creating music. Returning to Paynter's (1982: xiii) guiding principles, 'Music is a way of listening to sounds, and musical experience is primarily a way of *working* with sounds'. This is not to underestimate the power of listening; after all, 'the ear is the only "rule" that exists in music, and aural sensitivity is the key to all musical understanding' (1982: 126).

Figure 7.1 suggests a spiral structure for planning and assessment in music education which is built on these strands of learning (Fautley and Daubney, 2015: 6).

Four of these might be considered core inter-related musical activities – singing, playing, improvising and composing. Critical engagement and spiritual, moral, social and cultural (SMSC) underpin these. As Mills (2005: 158) reminds us, consolidation is very important:

> Performers do not make progress only by playing pieces that are more difficult technically, or faster, or longer. They show that they are getting better also by playing relatively easy pieces better than they did previously, or even just by revisiting pieces that they learnt previously, in order to consolidate them.

Mills (2005) also reminds us that learning is not necessarily linear; this is reflected in the spiral model (Figure 7.1) by the arrows in both directions:

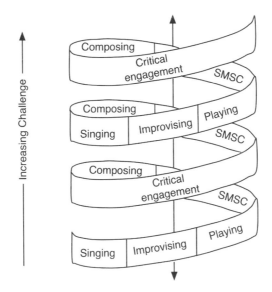

Figure 7.1   A planning and assessment spiral

Source: Fautley and Daubney (2015: 6)

Reprinted with permission from the Incorporated Society of Musicians and ISM Trust

> when something new comes along – a new instrument to play … or they
> engage as a listener with a whole new type of music … students may drop
> down by a couple of turns or so as they absorb this new experience.

Planning is part of a reflective and reflexive cyclic process examining the design and
effectiveness of the learning through constant questioning and the brokering of a
range of solutions. The planning cycle (Figure 7.2) works on a unit and individual
lesson basis, encouraging you to continually reflect on and act within and between
lessons. It reminds us that there is a range of learners within every class and that
opportunities need to be inclusive, motivating and relevant, building on children's
prior experiences and drawing together their musical lives inside and outside the
classroom. Differentiation is absolutely key to effective planning.

Co-constructing a curriculum

If we want children to be excited by learning, we should consider how to encourage them to have co-ownership of the construction of both planning and
assessment of their learning (Swann et al., 2012). This also helps us to understand
what they don't enjoy, what they would like more focus on, and to gather new
ideas. There are many ways in which their input could be gathered, but we should
also be aware that they don't know what they don't know. In other words, the
things they suggest are likely to reflect their own limited experiences. There are
clear benefits of including their ideas; returning to Smith et al.'s (2005) research
into what young people say motivates them, children are likely to have suggestions

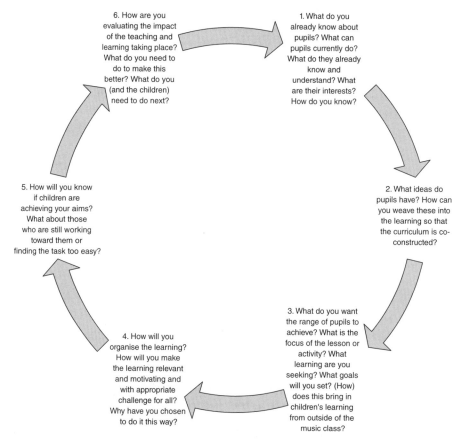

Figure 7.2 A reflective and reflexive planning cycle

which embrace their musical preferences, their preferred ways of learning music (which is likely to include collaborative learning with friends), and they are likely to prefer active first-hand learning opportunities. They are likely to suggest ideas that bring in ways in which they learn outside the classroom environment, particularly including learning music by ear and the use of music/mobile technologies.

There may also be other people to ask for ideas, advice and input, including other teachers, the music coordinator and any visiting music teachers. Having such a rich and diverse range of voices diversifies the musical influences brought into the classroom, as well as potentially improving access to live music.

Also remember that learning outside of the classroom environment is a two-way process. As well as bringing in ideas from outside, learning within the classroom will hopefully influence musical learning and engagement in the 'third environment' (Hargreaves et al., 2003) outside of the classroom.

Much of what you find out from pupils is likely to come from listening to them, discussions with them and creative ways which encourage honest dialogue. Taking an interest in pupils builds relationships and helps you know each other a little better. Moore (2012) suggests that relationship building encourages and facilitates dialogue rather than monologue. Productive dialogue and relationship building promote 'situational interest' (Urdan and Turner, 2007); children often become more motivated due to the interest and levels of engagement of the teacher or other important others.

Such approaches also help children to recognise where they are in their learning, what they might consider doing next and how they might go about it – the essence of formative developmental processes. You might also want to consider collecting ideas on Post-it notes or anonymously on screwed up bits of paper, and to create opportunities to bring back their ideas any time they want during the week, as we don't all have our best ideas right on the spot! Co-construction works if handled well because the decision-making power is shared and collaborative ownership ensues.

Planning for music across the early years

The Statutory Framework for the Early Years Foundation Stage (DfE, 2014a) only specifically mentions music under the heading 'Expressive Arts and Design'. This in itself is paradoxical; many of the ways young children access 'literacy', 'numeracy' and 'understanding the world' are through their on-going interactions with the world, which are entrenched in sounds. This includes playing games (including musical games), singing songs, chants and rhymes (including, for example, those that help with learning to count whilst children walk up steps) and making, changing and combining sounds as children go about exploring, constructing and understanding their environment and the relationships within it – both real and imaginary. Songs, chants and rhymes contribute to communication and language development. Listening and responding to music and stories through singing, playing, dancing and movement also contribute to physical development. Being a part of something musical, whether spontaneous or planned, contributes to children's personal, social and emotional development in multiple ways. Music is weaved through a young child's existence and contributes to their all-round development.

Specific early learning goals include the following (DfE, 2014b):

Exploring and using media and materials: children sing songs, make music and dance, and experiment with ways of changing them.

Being imaginative: children use what they have learnt about media and materials in original ways, thinking about uses and purposes. They represent their own ideas, thoughts and feelings through design and technology, art, music, dance, role-play and stories.

Planning for musical learning in the early years needs to take account of children's rapid emotional, social, physical and intellectual development across their first few years of life. Therefore, the planning needs to provide high quality experiences in a safe and nurturing environment that gives young children a balance between creative freedom and structure, in order to continually learn and develop through self-initiated and purposefully planned opportunities. There are plentiful ways of exploring with sounds, voices, simple technology and instruments. Skills require a particular level of physical dexterity; for example, small babies cannot physically hold and blow a recorder safely. Children's physical, emotional and social skills develop over time – for example, holding a beater and purposely striking individual notes on a glockenspiel, poking the teddy bear in the eye first. Individual children progress at different rates and we need to bear this in mind when we plan; observing what they do for themselves is an important step in planning a range of possibilities for 'where next' and providing opportunities for their exploration to flourish.

Planning in the early years often takes a very free-flowing approach, encouraging children to be able to walk in both worlds – self-initiated learning and exploration, and to engage willingly in more structured learning activities, moving seamlessly between them. Therefore, planning needs to reflect this and offer plentiful opportunities for children to create, explore, make, respond and critically engage with music in many different ways. One way to do this is to think through the desired outcomes for a particular time period and create a list of potential learning opportunities. An example is given in Table 7.1 (adapted from Bance, 2012).

Table 7.1 Example of music incorporated into an early years outline plan for one week

Theme for the week for the 3–5 group	Doctors and nurses		
Day	Focused learning opportunities	Self-initiated musical play and exploration	Notes/ feedback
Monday	Playing around with the voice in story time; moving like the characters	Choose and explore sounds and instruments in the themed space during free play Have microphones available, and dressing-up costumes in a doctor's bag Also have a bank of music and sounds recorded onto a portable device that the children can use independently, along with simple music technology for them to explore	
Tuesday	Using instruments, props and puppets to tell stories and perform songs, developing fine and gross motor skills		
Wednesday	Going for a sound walk and audio recording the sounds; live music from visiting parents		
Thursday	Activities that encourage spontaneous movement, expression, discussing feelings and acknowledging the feelings of others		
Friday	Playing musical games that involve turn-taking and the purposeful playing of instruments		

It is important to rotate the focus and type of activities on a particular day each week as many children are in childcare settings part-time. It is difficult to fit everything into one week, so over time planning should aim to cover a wide range of activities and learning opportunities which are both child-led and adult-led. However, as well as having a musical focus for the day, there are many other opportunities to weave music into daily activities. For example, there could be music for different routines such as clearing up, songs for counting, instruments and vocal exploration in stories, hello and goodbye songs that use children's names, music and movement, a sound garden or a role-play about music. There is great potential for music throughout every day, nourishing children's playfulness.

Some excellent advice on music in the early years is given in Bance's (2012) guidance for early years practitioners. The Sounds of Intent Early Years Framework (2015: 15) states that 'children engage with music in three different ways:

- Reactively – by listening and responding to what they hear;
- Proactively – by making sounds and music themselves; and
- Interactively – when musical engagement occurs with others.

Children may engage with all three different ways at once'.

TASK 7.2

If you work in an early years setting, look at your planning for one day and weave some musical opportunities throughout it.

Planning: some guiding principles

There is a danger that any lesson, regardless of the age group, can become just a set of nice activities without any thought about musical learning. There is also a danger that by over-planning the end point and what success might look like, the freedom to create and imagination are potentially inhibited. However, being aware of this minimises the risk. You could think of a plan as a map – having an idea of where you want to go (which may actually be a number of different destinations) and some possible ideas about the range of routes children might take to get there.

It may be that you are using a plan from a published scheme. Regardless of the source of the planning, you need to be aware of what learning you are seeking so that if the lesson is not working out for some reason – for example, the activities are too easy, too difficult or just plain dull – you can think up more appropriate and exciting ways to work towards the learning.

Table 7.2 offers a planning framework. It is a slight adaptation of the Framework for Assessment and Progression in Music Education (Daubney and Fautley,

Table 7.2 Planning framework for musical learning

	How does what you value appear in your curriculum?				
Being musical through:	**Desired differentiated skills**		**Pedagogic approaches to developing these skills**		**Desired differentiated**
Singing	What are the singing skills you aim to develop?		How will you develop these singing skills?		What is the knowledge and understanding of singing you are seeking to develop?
Playing	What are the playing skills you aim to develop?		How will you develop these playing skills?		What is the knowledge and understanding of playing you are seeking to develop?
Improvising	What are the improvising skills you aim to develop?	Why have you chosen these skills?	How will you develop these improvising skills?	Why have you chosen these pedagogies?	What is the knowledge and understanding of improvising you are seeking to develop?
Composing	What are the composing skills you aim to develop?		How will you develop these composing skills?		What is the knowledge and understanding of composing you are seeking to develop?
Critical engagement	What are the critical engagement skills you aim to develop?		How will you develop these critical engagement skills?		What is the knowledge and understanding involving critical engagement you are seeking to develop?
SMSC	What are the SMSC skills you aim to develop?		How will you develop these SMSC skills?		What is the knowledge and understanding involving SMSC you are seeking to develop?

Source: adapted from Daubney and Fautley (2014)

knowledge and understanding	Curricula materials			Assessment criteria	How does what you value appear in your assessment?		Assessed through communicating in and through music, evidenced through:				

How does what you value appear in your assessment?

knowledge and understanding

How will this knowledge and understanding of singing be developed?

How will this knowledge and understanding of playing be developed?

How will this knowledge and understanding of improvising be developed?

How will this knowledge and understanding of composing be developed?

How will this knowledge and understanding involving critical engagement be developed?

How will this knowledge and understanding involving SMSC be developed?

Curricula materials

Why have you chosen this range of knowledge and understanding?

What connections to pupils' wider knowledge and understanding are important?

What stimuli will be used, and what developmental materials will your pupils explore?

Why these units of work? Why in this order? Why these materials?

Assessment criteria

What are the assessment criteria you are using for singing?

What are the assessment criteria you are using for playing?

What are the assessment criteria you are using for improvising?

What are the assessment criteria you are using for composing?

What are the assessment criteria you are using for critical engagement?

What are the assessment criteria you are using for SMSC?

How, when and why are you using these in a formative, developmental fashion?

(How, when and why do you use these in a summative fashion?)

Assessed through communicating in and through music, evidenced through:

Responding

Creating and making

Talking

Exploring

Notating

How, when and why are you using these in a formative, developmental fashion?

(How, when and why are you using these in a summative fashion?)

2014; Fautley and Daubney, 2015). The framework is essentially a series of questions about planning and assessment. The questions are based around the musical learning sought and considered through the lens of musical and creative engagement via the first-hand musical activities of singing, composing, improvising, performing and critical engagement. The framework encourages thought about some of the other learning sought relating to spiritual, moral, social and cultural (SMSC) education. An overarching question asks how our values are embodied through the curriculum, delivery and assessment.

How to use the framework

The first thing to note is that the skills, knowledge and understanding are artificially separated, as are the key activities such as singing, improvising, etc. This is just to provide a comprehensive framework to help you think through what you are trying to do and achieve. Learning does not happen in such a fragmented way; musical learning is holistic, and the skills, knowledge and understanding developed will be bound up in what you do and how you go about it. Likewise, the assessment is integral to the planning; this is discussed further in Chapter 8.

In the first instance, you will probably plan individual one-off music lessons that may be part of a unit. Over time, this may develop into planning for a whole unit or across a whole year or Key Stage. The same planning framework will help you to plan on both a micro (individual lesson) and macro (unit or yearly plan) level.

In general, there are two ways in which curriculum planning happens. Whichever way you plan, you need to consider where these children are in their learning to be able to recognise and build on this. The two main approaches are summarised as:

1. Decide on the musical skills, knowledge and understanding that you want to develop, and how you will do this.
2. From one or more stimuli materials (e.g. a children's book, a topic about recycling or folk songs from a local collection), define the musical skills, knowledge and understanding that you hope to nurture and, from this, plan the musical learning experiences.

Leading on from this detailed thinking about the development of the curriculum and other learning opportunities, you should be able to define the success criteria. These may be related to some or all of the musical activities (singing, playing, improvising, composing, listening), but may also include other possible outcomes such as those related to social, moral, spiritual and cultural education.

Table 7.3 An example of desired unit outcomes

In this unit of work, pupils will learn:

Singing: to sing confidently as a class, developing their awareness of technical factors such as holding the notes, pronunciation and awareness of phrases/breathing, as well as developing the accuracy of pitch and rhythm.

Playing: to play new chords on the ukulele, working towards performing a song as a class. Pupils will also practise changing between chords, developing their dexterity, accuracy and speed.

Improvising: to try out their own strumming patterns.

Composing: to compose their own chorus of a song about life on the sea.

Critical engagement: to aurally identify simple chord changes when listening to music. Pupils will critique the work from listening to informal class recordings, making suggestions to improve the 'togetherness' of the ensemble.

SMSC: to work effectively in a group, which relies on listening to and respecting other people's ideas and suggestions. Pupils will also explore the cultural context of the music and imagine what it would be like to be at sea for weeks on end.

A worked example of the planning

Gill, a teacher at a village school in Cornwall, is planning a 45-minute lesson for her Year 4/5 class as part of an 8-week unit, which has a broad focus on the development of ensemble skills. The class has been working around a theme of 'pirates' across all subjects. This is the first lesson in the unit. Gill has been given a unit plan with desired outcomes for development across the unit (see Table 7.3).

There are many different ways you could approach the learning in this first lesson of the unit. Your entry point will depend on your knowledge of the class's musical experiences and prior achievements. First of all, you need to decide what your focus is in this lesson. Ideally, learning across the lesson should be focused towards this desired learning goal. For example, if the desired learning in the lesson is that pupils will develop their awareness of phrasing, of breathing when singing, and their ensemble skills, the warm-up or starter activity should have this focus, as well as the activities throughout the rest of the lesson.

Lesson planning is often slow in the early days of teaching – this is unsurprising and not something you should worry about. The plan should have enough detail for you to use it as a working document, yet leave flexibility and breathing space within the lesson for the unexpected to emerge.

An example of three linked lesson plans is shown in Figure 7.3. These plans are annotated to help you understand the reasons behind the choices made.

TASK 7.3

1. Using the reflective and reflexive learning cycle (Figure 7.2) and what you know already about the unit of work, decide on a focus for this first lesson. Remember that it should not include everything, for example your focus might be on just singing or singing and ukulele playing, or else it might be on improvising or composing or improvising *and* composing. The choice is yours.

2. Having decided on the focus, use the Planning and Assessment Framework (Figure 7.3) to identify the skills, knowledge and understanding that you wish pupils to develop in this lesson. It is helpful to think about this before you plan activities, as the planning then has a learning focus, rather than just being a nice set of fun activities which don't necessarily lead to any learning.

3. Identify some possible resources/materials.

4. What is the historical, cultural and social significance of the area of work you are exploring? What might you want to draw out of the learning in relation to this? How will you do this in ways that emerge from the music itself?

5. Think about how you will go about constructing the learning. What will you do and how will you do it? What will the children do? How will you introduce things? What will your role be?

6. How will the lesson starter draw children in? How will it consolidate and build on what they know already and also contribute to the desired learning? How will the main part of the lesson unfold? What will you share with children, and what will you let them discover for themselves? How will you draw the learning together towards the end of the lesson? How long will each part reasonably take?

7. Are there ways in which you can use audio and video recording to enhance the learning experiences?

8. Thinking about the children in your class, what can you do to differentiate the learning to provide an appropriate level of challenge and scaffolding for all pupils?

9. Share your lesson ideas with someone else and let them comment and contribute.

10. Put yourself in the shoes of three different children in your class. How will they feel about this lesson? Does it fit with their expectations, and are they likely to be motivated by the lesson content and approaches? Does the lesson help them to link learning together in order to see the relevance?

Music 2 Examples of planning

The following three lesson plans are provided as examples of planning in music. They do not contain the detail you will probably wish to have on your plans but do illustrate some of the points discussed previously.

Lesson One

Subject/topic: Do you believe in magic?	Date: 23/9/2016 Time: 1.15 p.m.	Teaching group/set: Y5 – mixed ability class No. of pupils: 28

Intended learning:	NC reference/context:
Children will learn to: • create musical soundscapes from a given starting point • critique their work through the cyclic use of audio-based recording.	Improvising, performing, creativity, playing instruments Links to literacy, drama and visual arts

Success criteria:	Assessment strategy:
All children will be able to: • select appropriate sounds for the musical purpose and explain why they were chosen • perform with appropriate control and awareness of the audience. Some children will be able to: • successfully combine and adapt sounds, justifying their choices of sounds and relating these effectively to the purpose/image.	• Observation, probing questions and listening during rehearsal, performances and discussion • Making aural recordings and playing back; listening to pupils discussing their own work

Key vocabulary:	Resources:	Risk assessment:
mood, texture, timbre, feeling, dynamics, start, stop, rest, silence, improvise	*Leon and the Place Between* by Angela McAllister Copies of pictures from the book Range of tuned and non-tuned percussion instruments, plus children's own instruments Video recording capability (e.g. mobile phone, flip camera, iPad)	Clear the space so that children can work on an uncluttered floor

Time	Teacher focus	Pupil focus
10 mins	Stunning starter – dim the lights, draw curtains. Teacher (in costume) to read the opening of the story. Hot-seating – pupils ask questions of 'Leon'. Finish with a discussion on words to describe the mood.	Pupils seated together on the floor, room laid out as a performing space. Pair and share – think up interesting questions to ask Leon/the magician. One sticky note each – write words that describe the mood set. Share. Think about the kind of music that would be needed to accompany each scene. Share ideas with the class.

It is often useful to 'hook' musical learning around a source, e.g. a picture, book or song.

It is important to encourage children's musical lives from beyond the classroom into your classroom work.

Classroom layout is important. Have the class standing together in a bunch of people or a horseshoe.

(Continued)

Figure 7.3 (Continued)

10 mins	Join in with whole-class improvisation based on an image from the book.	Thinking of the words written down, which part of the image do these go with?
	Put up the image on the whiteboard screen.	Taking a musical instrument, 60 seconds to explore the different and unusual sounds it can make.
	Record the resulting soundscape. Take suggestions for cues to start/stop.	Focusing on the different parts of the picture (as the frame moves around) try to add in the sounds together to create a soundscape.
20 mins	Split pupils into groups – support groups to create, perform and critique the effectiveness of their own work.	Working in groups of four pupils, each group will have a different image from the book to create music to 'tell the story' (no more than 1 minute per group). 3 mins – discuss ideas, 5 mins – try them out and refine, one group to perform 'work in progress', share ideas for improvement then continue to develop.
20 mins	Direct a performance of the whole book. Make recording to share. Lead discussion/critiquing of work.	Each group to perform their soundscape while they tell the story. Video this. Watch the video back and critique the work, each group commenting on their own intentions and others commenting on whether these were met.

Really important that the teacher joins in/models/demonstrates.

Exploring the instrument with a critical mass of noise going on is a useful strategy to overcome fear of failure. Make sure the class know the cue to stop exploring and praise them for adhering to this.

The mini plenary is a great way to move work on for the whole class when groups are working independently – it encourages children to reflect upon, discuss their work and find solutions.

Ofsted urge the use of video/audio as part of the musical process and to show progress over time as part of a sound-based portfolio.

Developing the quality by rehearsing parts/techniques etc., not just singing through from beginning to end, is extremely important.

Lesson Two

Subject/topic:	Date: 30/9/2016	Teaching group/set: Y5 – mixed ability class
What kind of magic?	Time: 10.30 a.m.	No. of pupils: 28

Intended learning:	NC reference/context:
Children will learn to: • respond to music through art, using this as a prompt to discuss thoughts and feelings about music heard • rehearse and develop the quality of singing through learning new material aurally.	Rehearsing, singing, performing, creativity, listening and responding to music, discussing music Links to visual arts

Success criteria:	Assessment strategy:
All children will be able to: • memorise most lyrics and sections of melody of a new song; perform broadly in tune and time • respond to music through art and give reasons for choices with basic use of technical language. Some children will be able to: • sing with appropriate posture, good diction, tuning and sense of timing; be aware of others in the group and fit their voice in appropriately • ask astute and interesting questions about the music, justify their thoughts and feelings using sophisticated language to communicate their ideas effectively.	• Listening to pupils discussing their thoughts about the music • Listening, watching while children are singing without the pupils realising you are listening

Key vocabulary:	Resources:	Risk assessment:
singing, warm up, diction, tuning, soundscape, dynamics	Recorded music based upon a circus/magic/wonder theme Song materials (may include recording, lyrics on IWB) Evocative visual image	Clear area for working; no electric cables running across the floor

Time	Teacher focus	Pupil focus
15 mins	Lead/co-lead an interactive vocal warm-up which also incorporates movement. Help pupils to create a whole-class vocal soundscape of a new image of awe/wonder/magic. Use a 'picture frame' of folded paper to isolate parts of the picture. Teacher should join in.	Warm up bodies and voices. Focus on the sound production and following the 'leader'. Pupils to respond to the changing images through vocal improvisation, body percussion and sounds from the environment. Think about which parts of the images will be loudest/softest and adjust their sounds accordingly.
20 mins	Teacher directs pupils to respond through drawing to the music extracts played. Be sure to explain in advance that there are no right/wrongs – also that they will be 'asking interesting questions' about the music. Use probing questions, particularly around 'why'.	Pupils respond to the two short extracts through drawing. In groups of four, discuss their own images and reasons with each other and then think up two really interesting questions about the music they would like to ask another group about the music. Bring two groups together to share questions and responses.
25 mins	Teach the whole class a song based upon the theme of circus/awe/wonder/ fantasy worlds, e.g. 'Magical Mystery Tour' (Beatles), 'Sound of Silence' (Simon & Garfunkel), 'It's a Kind of Magic' (Queen). Lead the rehearsal of different parts to improve the quality, based upon children's suggestions.	Pupils learn song, probably the chorus first. Rehearse parts to improve the quality – particularly phrasing, diction, beginning and endings (as opposed to singing through without working on any parts). Pupils make performing suggestions/lead sections. Make a video recording of an 'in progress' performance of the song at the end of the lesson to use in the next lesson; write a suggestion for improvement on a sticky note bank as they leave.

Pupils might help to lead this. This strategy also takes away the focus from the teacher.

Make sure children know what they will need to do before they listen to the music. This engages them as critical listeners with a purpose, rather than springing questions on them afterwards.

Listen in on the questions asked – these are at least as enlightening as the responses to the questions!

Find a strategy for teaching a song that you feel comfortable with.

Lesson Three

Subject/topic:	Date: 7/10/2016	Teaching group/set: Y5
Rapping magic!	Time: 1.15 p.m.	No. of pupils: 28

Intended learning:	NC reference/context:
Children will learn to: • construct and refine lyrics for an 8-bar rap 'break' • perform in a rap style and practise keeping in time.	Rehearsing, refining, inventing, performing, critiquing, creativity Links to literacy and visual arts

Success criteria:	Assessment strategy:
All children will be able to: • suggest lyrics and key phrases for a short rap 'break' • perform broadly in time. Some children will be able to: • sequence the lyrics to make an interesting, coherent and musically satisfying rap 'break' • perform the rap section with a good sense of timing, metre and vocal clarity.	• Observation of children working on development of rap and in rehearsal/performance and negotiating with each other about content • Listening to the discussions and questioning • Taking suggestions for improvement based upon comments from the video in the previous lesson

You might also take a suggestion from the children about this – it is best to do this in the previous week so that you have time to prepare it.

Links to the NC requirement to use voices in different ways.

(Continued)

Figure 7.3 (Continued)

Key vocabulary:		Resources:	Risk assessment:
rap, metre, timing, break, chorus, verse, structure, rhyming, rhythm		Paper and pens	No trailing cables, clear area for working
		Song materials	
		Looped track at 60 beats per minute	
		Images drawn by the children in the previous lesson	

Time	Teacher focus	Pupil focus
15 mins	Scaffold the conversations. Teacher to write these on whiteboard. Lead a very short vocal warm up then facilitate the singing of the song with a focus on improvement.	Working in teams of four, each group to come up with their 'top tip' for improvement (what to improve and suggestions for how to do this) based upon the video from the end of previous lesson. Sing through the song, trying to implement the suggestions made by other pupils.
10 mins	Teacher extracts information on 'what makes a good rap' by modelling/demonstrating/for a range of good/not so good ideas. Teacher writes list based upon pupils' suggestions. Model the process of constructing a 4-line rap (8-bar), showing ideas of different rhyming structures.	Pupils make suggestions about what makes a good rap and make suggestions to improve things they feel could be better/write the next line from the demonstrations.
30 mins	Teacher facilitates groups to write their own short raps. TA to support pupils with the literacy as required. Teacher should oversee the scribing, rehearsal and performances, make video recording for use at the start of the following lesson (where all of these parts will start to come into one arrangement).	Based on the pictures of the previous week and the post-it note words from lesson 1, pupils work in groups of four to create an 8-bar rap (this is likely to be 4 lines) about one of the fantasy worlds and linked broadly with the theme of the song learnt. 'Phone a friend' if needing a line finishing. 'Rehearse, perform and record.

Figure 7.3 Planning the primary national curriculum

From Sewell (2015) *Planning the Primary National Curriculum*, London: Sage.

Marginal notes (left):

You can easily make one of these on a program such as AcidXpress or Soundation, or using the pre-recorded loops on an electronic keyboard.

What to improve AND how to do this are key points relating to good practice in promoting developmental feedback.

'Good' modelling and 'bad' modelling both offer opportunities for children to see what is possible and make suggestions.

Get everyone to share their first line, then the first 2 lines – this offers plenty of opportunity for peer feedback and suggestions and keeps the momentum going.

The modelling should have made it clear to the children that there is a great deal of creative freedom and that they can put their own individual 'stamp' on this.

Marginal notes (right):

This mic necessa performe the who class – might m their ow informal recordin use in th following lesson.

Provide children home-m paper 'c wear wh they per watch he changes mood of performa due to providin little mo authenti

Unit planning

When planning for units of work, the same thinking processes are followed. As with individual lesson planning, it is helpful and necessary to think about and identify the learning sought by the end of the unit and plan backwards from there. Remember that this end point does not always have to be a performance – there are many ways of sharing and celebrating work. This can be during the unit as well as at the end; there may not necessarily be a big 'end point' for each unit. For example, you may wish to share recordings of children's work, or to have a meaningful event that links with the work.

In both of the following examples, the music has a specific and real-life purpose, which is more suitable in these particular cases than what you may traditionally think of as the end of a unit. Within your planning, you can be as ingenious as you like in helping children to find ways to develop, critique and share their work.

Scenario 1

In a cross-curricular unit on animation and film, Year 5 pupils have created their own zoetrope in the art lessons. Using a loop-based application on the class set of tablet computers, they have been composing their own dance tracks in music lessons in order to accompany the movement of the zoetrope, thinking about the mood of the characters in their animation. In this particular lesson, the children have set up tables in the school hall as 'animation stations', with four pupils at each table. Each child in turn plays their music and spins the zoetrope. The others at the table, playing the part of the 'director', watch and listen, deciding on how effective the music is for the images and deciding on two questions that they would like to ask the composer about the music in order to generate discussion and feedback.

Scenario 2

Year 6 has been undertaking a song-writing unit, exploring the many ways into song writing. Together, pupils have written a leaving song for Mrs Caines, their reception teacher who is retiring after many years of service. The Year 6 teacher organises for the class to visit a nearby secondary school and record the song professionally in the school studio. The music teacher in the secondary school creates some instrumental tracks, recorded in advance by members of the secondary school big band. Six of the pupils from the primary school who play the cello or guitar go along to join in with this instrumental work, playing simple parts learnt on the day. The finished recording is given to all pupils on a CD to take home. It is also used to teach the song to all of the other children in the school. Simple choreography is worked out and this is also learnt by the whole school without the knowledge of Mrs Caines. On the last day of the school year, the children surprise Mrs Caines as she carries out her final break duty. The song is played over the PA system into the playground and, little by little, as the music starts up, children and staff join in with the singing and dancing, creating a flash mob in honour of their teacher.

Long-term planning

Long-term planning encourages us to think about what we seek to develop across a sustained period of time such as a Key Stage or a school year. It is not just a series of units that can be taught in an interchangeable order; it is underpinned by defined skills, knowledge, understanding, habits, behaviours and attitudes introduced in the order and fashion of our choosing. Swapping around the order of the units is fine, so long as we recognise the need to adapt the desired learning and expectations too as they have taken place at a different point in the sequence of learning. Like all plans, long-term plans are dynamic, not fixed, and will need updating and revising at regular intervals.

Reflecting on planning

Developing reflective habits is considered crucial to teaching in order to continually advance our professional knowledge and, ultimately, to develop better quality learning (Pollard et al., 2014). Kemmis (1985: 141) describes the act of reflection as:

> ... a dialectical process: it looks inwards at our thoughts and thought processes and outward at the situation in which we find ourselves; when we consider the interaction of the internal and external, our reflection orients us for further thought and action. Reflection is thus 'meta thinking' (thinking about thinking) in which we consider the relationship between our thoughts and action in a particular context.

In other words, being a reflective practitioner has the potential to permeate everything we do. Just as we hope to encourage learners to cognitively engage with learning processes (Chapter 2), we too should strive for this same level of awareness within our teaching, particularly considering the impact on children's learning. Reflecting during and after lessons – using our teacher radar – helps us to notice the world around us as we observe it unfolding. This allows us to make informed decisions to adapt what we do or how we do it, through reading social situations and evolving events, in order to adapt our actions and teaching with the aim of improving learning experiences for pupils.

Early career teachers sometimes get bound up in reflecting predominantly on behaviour in lessons. Whilst this is important, we need to look past this to reflect on the learning in relation to the aims and learning sought for a lesson and for individual children. What is your own evaluation of the lesson and the learning from it (yours and your pupils')? What has formed the basis of these decisions? What adaptations do you feel it would be beneficial to make next time, and also how will you use this to feed into the planning and delivery of the next lesson? This might relate to many things – for example, the activities, the pace of learning, the relationships, the ways you introduce things, the way you set up the learning environment. The trick here is to be future orientated – it is good to think about and analyse the events of the past, but focus on practical and positive ways to identify how you will adapt things in the future. Additionally, just as with children's learning, teachers develop over time and it is very encouraging to look back and recognise your development, considering the ways you think as well as act. Occasionally, lessons don't go to plan and have the potential to get us down and diminish our self-worth as a teacher. When this happens, find a moment to look back on and celebrate your development over a period of time and then think about future possible adaptations.

Reflection is about both feelings and thoughts. As Williams (2002: 55, cited in Paige-Smith and Craft, 2011: 17) states: 'It [reflective practice] allows us to integrate the technical expertise of the professional with the personal and emotional qualities of the individual … allow[ing] our natural instincts to interact with a professional approach.'

Reflection coupled with reflexivity is therefore our desired goal.

Chapter summary

Planning is a crucial part of developing enriching musical learning experiences. It is enhanced when teachers know their pupils well and are able to draw on their own strengths and confidence to create learning experiences and opportunities within and beyond the classroom that are motivating, relevant and build on what children can already do, as well as what they know and understand. Planning has the potential to bring depth and meaning to children's education, recognising the dynamic state of society and the school learning community. Through constant dialogue with and between others in the learning community (particularly pupils), we can create powerful learning contexts which really listen to and embrace children's perspectives and interests. Our personal interactions with pupils are fundamentally important to their development – planning is therefore multi-dimensional and complex, encompassing so much more than just the activities we aim to lead.

There are many stages to planning and whilst, on the one hand, it may appear to be a 'recipe' for creating a lesson or unit of work, you need to remember that, in the end, it is a flexible thinking framework that needs to live and breathe, giving room for children's ideas, input and creativity. Focusing on the learning and outcomes sought from the unit and lessons within it (i.e. the big picture stuff) helps to provide a structural framework for your ideas and ensures that learning is planned for, not just hoped for!

The internet is packed with lesson plans of varying quality and your school may well buy into or use a published scheme. Ultimately, though, the best planning is that over which we have personal ownership, so that we know that it is suitable for what we want and for the children we are working with. In this sense, planning is a dynamic process as no two classes are ever identical, and in order to personalise the learning we need to know the quirks, culture, friendships and experiences within and beyond the classroom. We also need to work hard to help children to recognise and make links between home, school and the rest of the world; it is all too easy to see a unit of work as a self-contained entity.

We all cherry pick and adapt ideas from other people – after all, why re-invent the wheel? Over time you will get more adept at critiquing other people's ideas in order to work out what is best for your class, which ideas are brilliant and which should be avoided. The problem with using planning from online and published sources is that you do not necessarily understand the thought behind it, the context in which it was developed for use and the prior experiences or expectations of any of the children for which it was written. Just because it is available does not mean it is any good! Creating your own differentiated planning, with guidance and advice from others including the children, and listening to and acting on your own honest, on-going developmental feedback, is the best way to plan. It gives you ownership, autonomy and understanding of the decisions you make within your own unique context and a springboard for reflective and reflexive practice.

Further reading

Daubney, A. and Fautley, M. (2014) *The National Curriculum for Music: An Assessment and Progression Framework*. London: Incorporated Society of Musicians (ISM). Available online via www.ism.org/nationalcurriculum

Daubney, A. and Mackrill, D. (2015) Planning music in the National Curriculum. In K. Sewell (ed.) *Planning the Primary National Curriculum*. London: Sage.

Fautley, M. and Daubney, A. (2015) *The National Curriculum for Music: A Framework for Curriculum, Pedagogy and Assessment in Key Stage 3 Music*. London: Incorporated Society of Musicians (ISM). Available at: www.ism.org/images/files/ISM_A_Framework_for_Curriculum,_Pedagogy_and_Assessment_KS3_Music_WEB.pdf

Paige-Smith, A. and Craft, A. (2011) *Developing Reflective Practice in the Early Years*. Maidenhead: Open University Press.

8

MAKING ASSESSMENT MUSICAL

It is important to recognize at the outset that assessment in education has various functions, each distinctive and requiring distinctive tactics and methods ... Once diverse assessment functions are identified, the press towards a universal one-size-fits-all approach to assessment diminishes, a more complex view of assessment emerges, and the options one can consider expand. These issues and possibilities are as germane to assessment in the arts as they are to assessment in other fields. (Eisner, 1996: 4)

Introduction

Eisner reminds us about the importance, relevance and universality of assessment, yet also the need to take a broad view of meaningful assessment in the arts. Chapter 7 explored the processes of planning alongside the place of reflective and reflexive practice across teaching and learning. Assessment is integral to these processes. However, where assessment gets involved, the waters often start to become muddied. Assessment in schools is controversial and highly emotive. When we think of assessment, our immediate thoughts may well spring to the statutory testing of children at various ages in their educational lives. According to Alexander (2010: 497), 'primary pupils [in England] are tested more frequently and at an earlier age than most other countries'. As Butler (1987: 475) laments, ranking children's grades undermines collaboration: 'the normative grades prevalent in schools seem a clear example of information that focuses attention on the self by emphasizing outcome and social comparison, or both, rather than process or task mastery.'

In this sense, the word 'assessment' has been hijacked. When used well, assessment is an essential and powerful part of children's musical learning journeys, yet it is sometimes responsible for more damage than it does good (Harlen and Deakin Crick, 2002). This chapter considers the purposes and roles of assessment in music education, identifying ways in which it can be authentically and purposefully used to enhance and promote musical learning.

Objectives

Through this chapter you will:

- explore assessment and how it can be used to promote musical learning and progression
- recognise the importance of formative, developmental assessment
- consider some of the challenges of assessment in music education.

Holistic assessment: learning from practice in the early years

Practitioners working across the early years continually observe children's behaviours, attitudes and specific learning goals, as outlined in the Early Years Framework (DfE, 2014a). Little formal reporting is required: a short 'progress check' for children aged between 24 and 36 months and then completion of the 'early years profile' at the end of the school year in which the child is 5 years old. At this point, a judgement must be made about whether a child meets a particular learning goal, is working towards it or exceeding it. This takes into account evidence from parents, practitioners and the child themselves (DfE, 2014a).

Since the goals themselves are holistic, judgements are formed on the basis of observing and recording 'evidence' across a wide variety of learning situations and extended time periods. Some helpful guidance from this document (DfE, 2014a: 13) notes:

> On-going assessment (also known as formative assessment) is an integral part of the learning and development process. It involves practitioners observing children to understand their level of achievement, interests and learning styles, and to then shape learning experiences for each child reflecting those observations. In their interactions with children, practitioners should respond to their own day-to-day observations about children's progress and observations that parents and carers share.

It goes on to state:

> Assessment should not entail prolonged breaks from interaction with children, nor require excessive paperwork. Paperwork should be limited to that which is absolutely necessary to promote children's successful learning and development.

Many children leave their early years settings with a portfolio of their development over their time in the early years setting, comprising photographs and physical examples of their work, and with audio/video recordings of them singing or playing musical instruments, telling stories, being part of role-plays and exploring their world inside and beyond the classroom. This rich evidence source allows parents an insight into their child's learning world and celebrates their achievements. It also validates judgements from early years professionals about the extent to which the early years goals have been met.

It is absolutely clear that there is an integral relationship between curriculum, pedagogy and assessment. Assessment of music in early years settings is not based around tests or specific tasks; instead, it is integral to children's unfolding learning and open-ended development. We should not fall into the trap of thinking open-ended equals unplanned. A high degree of planning happens so that children thrive in the early years, exploring music in guided ways alongside those initiated by the children. It is interesting to note the shifting balance of child-initiated learning:

> Practitioners must respond to each child's emerging needs and interests, guiding their development through warm, positive interaction. As children grow older, and as their development allows, it is expected that the balance will gradually shift towards more activities led by adults, to help children prepare for more formal learning, ready for Year 1. (DfE, 2014a: 9)

It is noticeable that the shift towards adult-led activity and formal learning starts to get in the way of musical learning and muddies the waters in relation to the term 'assessment'. Assessment is sometimes incorrectly thought of as the thing we do 'at the end' of learning, i.e. assessing the 'outcome' of whatever the task is. Yet, Swanwick's (1999: 71) mantra – 'to teach is to assess' – indicates the power of assessment throughout teaching and learning.

Ross et al. (1993: xi) point out that 'the word assess is derived from the Latin ad + sedere, meaning to "sit down together"', thereby endorsing collaborative approaches. Black and Wiliam (1998: 2) offer the following definitions:

> The term 'assessment' refers to all those activities undertaken by teachers, and by their students in assessing themselves, which provide information to be used as feedback to modify the teaching and learning activities in which they are engaged. Such assessment becomes 'formative assessment' when the evidence is actually used to adapt the teaching work to meet the needs.

The importance of getting assessment right

Assessments influence how people feel about themselves and their abilities. It is sadly the case that many people make harsh judgements about themselves in relation to the arts. These judgements come, in part, from constant interactions with other people – body language, comments, eye contact, smiles, dialogue (or even silence), and not just from grades awarded. As Swanwick (1999: 67) says, 'there can be no teaching in any real sense of that word without sensitive and responsive assessment'. Assessment is a significant part of your armoury – useful to you as a teacher and to your pupils but also with the potential to be destructive.

Language is extremely powerful in any context; our choice of words (or no words) and the tone used are cues that people interpret within their own belief system. Being alert and mindful, reading situations in the classroom well and constantly being aware of your impact on individuals and groups, are crucial.

Awarding grades or marks is also fraught with difficulty – these perpetuate the feelings that children (or adults) have about themselves as musicians and learners. Grades and marks 'will emphasise ability and competition with others' (Butler, 1987: 475), encouraging a culture of comparison. For some children, this may be motivating, particularly if they are achieving well and continually get awarded high marks. For others though, the grades and marks give rise to negative feelings about themselves, their abilities and their progress.

For all of these reasons, 'formal' assessment in primary music should be as hands off and as light touch as possible. Assessment is, however, fundamentally important to planning, teaching and learning. It is a question of what you do with it, how and when it is utilised and whom it is for.

TASK 8.1

Think about the following scenarios in the music classroom. Consider how they would make you feel if you were a pupil.

Year 5 is rehearsing a song about the Romans for assembly, singing along with a backing track. The class is singing generally in time and in tune. Pupils often join in late with the first line of the verses and some of the verse lyrics are mumbled, but choruses are sung with gusto. As the song nears the end, Miss Atkinson stops the recording and converses with the class.

Scenario A

Miss Atkinson, shaking her head and looking generally disgruntled: 'If I've told you once, I've told you a hundred times. You need to sing out more, project your voices. You're very lazy about pronouncing the words properly – how is the rest of the school going to understand what you're singing about if you keep mumbling all the time? We're singing about Gladiators here. Not just 'a-tors'. Gladiators. Gla-di-a-tors. Stand up straight and concentrate. Repeat after me. Gla-di-a-tors are the stron-gest figh-ters in the Ro-man land.'

Scenario B

Miss Atkinson, smiling and looking around at the class: 'Well done, Year 5, you've really started to get to grips with the words and it's quite a tricky song, isn't it? The choruses sound brilliant and you're all joining in really well. Before we finish for today, let's just have a look at the words in the verses to make them even clearer. Let's all make sure our mouth muscles are really working hard to pronounce all of the long words really clearly. To warm up our mouth muscles a little, let's pretend we're chewing gum. [*The class copies*]. Now I'll say a line and you repeat it. Hilary, count us in please. [*Hilary counts 1-2-3-4*]. <u>Gla</u>-di-a-tors are the stron-gest figh-ters in the Ro-man land.' [*Miss Atkinson over-emphasises the beginning of the word Gladiators and the class repeats the phrase*].

Assessing in the here and now

In a classroom situation, a teacher is always scanning the horizon, looking at and listening for what is unfolding, working out where children are in their learning, what they have grasped easily, what misconceptions they have, how they might be stuck on something, and so much more. This kind of iterative, on-going assessment forms the basis of many of the decisions we make in the here and now; observations inform our understanding of what we see and hear in the classroom and they help us to plan our next move through critical self-questioning: 'Should I intervene and ask a question to get them back on track? Should I stop the class? Should we practise that phrase again in order to reinforce the lyrics? Do I need to give John something more challenging – is he off-task because the task is too easily achievable? I can see Tiago is speeding up so perhaps I should go and stand next to him and play along to try and keep the tempo steady.'

It is this constant assessment that drives the decisions we make in the moment. What we see and hear also helps us to form judgements and opinions (sometimes unhelpfully) about pupils. This reflection/action loop also guides our actions across sustained periods of time. It helps us to answer questions that continually inform our planning. Critical questions include (but are not limited to):

- What was really successful, perhaps more successful than I (or the children) expected? Why?
- Are there any concepts, skills, ideas that the class, groups or individuals struggled to grasp? Why?
- What are the next steps needed to guide the learning process?
- What needs revising? For instance, content, approaches, classroom layout, pace, groupings?
- How can I challenge the pupils to take more ownership of their own learning?
- What feedback is needed in order to help specific children/groups improve? Who is best placed to lead this, how and when?
- How should I structure the next lesson?
- What skills should be introduced/developed next? How might that be done? What knowledge and understanding does this assume?
- What were my judgements based on?
- Were these valid and fair and how does what we learnt (both me as the teacher and the pupils) impact on what happens next?

Who are assessments for?

The most significant reason for assessing is to help you and the pupils to continually develop musically and in other ways, through a wide range of flexible, worthwhile and relevant learning situations. Constant interaction and developmental frameworks allow children to work out where they are in their learning, the possibilities of what they might do next and how this might happen. This is the essence of formative, developmental assessment; when used well, it builds trust, confidence, a sense of musical community and a musical culture.

Inevitably, assessment is also for others beyond the teacher and pupils. School 'systems' (a term coined by Fautley, 2010) expect regular numerical data to be provided, particularly for core subjects, although thankfully in music in primary school this is not usually required and long may it stay that way! Within primary music education, there is no place for pupils to be aware of grades, marks or ranking systems that encourage comparisons with others.

Parents/carers also receive 'reports' about their child. This normally comes in the form of a written report, once or twice a year. The opportunities for remarks on music within this are usually minimal and confined to a very short tokenistic comment. More recently, there seems to be a move towards tick boxes where judgements are made about whether a child is 'performing' at, below or above an arbitrary (and, often, ill-defined or non-defined) expected standard. It is impossible to sum up the richness of a child's musical life and learning through one sentence from a comments bank.

Parent/carer consultation evenings held during a school year are also potentially rich opportunities to discuss and show a child's musical journey through recordings and other examples of work, and many children get involved in music events in the wider school and community. These provide a great chance for families to celebrate and share children's musical lives.

Creating assessment goals

The planning framework introduced in Chapter 7 is also useful for helping frame ideas about what it might be useful to assess. The question 'what criteria are you using to assess?' relates to the 'activities' of singing, playing, composing, improvising and listening. Assessment 'evidence' is gathered through observing children as they go about making, creating and responding to music, and also from discussion, listening to them talking, recordings, notated scores, notes and anything else related to their engagement with music. Evidence should be gathered over extended periods of time, not in 'assessment moments'. It should also take into account all of a child's musical life, not just the time in the classroom in a particular unit of work.

As advocated by the early years guidance for assessment, holistic goals work well across primary (and secondary) education too. For example, one holistic target at the end of a particular year and for a particular child might be: 'Suggest, follow and lead simple performance directions.'

At the end of the learning period and based on a variety of 'evidence', the teacher need simply mark whether this particular child is:

- 'working towards' this target (−)
- 'working at' this target (=), or
- 'working beyond' this target (+).

It is useful to identify a small number of holistic goals for children in your class – there is likely to be some similarity in the goals for different members of the same class. Not having only one 'set' target for all children personalises the learning so that the culture is about celebrating development and achievement, otherwise some children may always be 'working towards' unrealistic targets (for which the term 'failure' may potentially be perceived). This means that all children can either 'meet' or 'exceed' their goals, which, if they have to be shared, is surely better for their self-esteem.

Table 8.1 shows an example of the long-term goals for two different Year 3 pupils, Eddie and Jack.

Development towards these long-term holistic goals is sought through evidence across the whole of the chosen period, for example a school year. To help understand and develop the assessment criteria across extended periods of time, Figure 8.1 provides some exemplar statements (Daubney and Fautley, 2014: 6–7). Note that these are not age related and they are purposely not linked (e.g. A6 is not necessarily related to B6, C6 and D6), as musical development is not always linear and cannot be satisfactorily reduced to an over-simplistic, generalisable framework.

Table 8.1 Examples of long-term goals for different pupils

Eddie	Jack
1. Sing and play confidently, maintaining an appropriate pulse	1. Sing in tune within a limited pitch range, maintaining an approximate pulse
2. Maintain an independent part in a small group when playing or singing (e.g. rhythm, ostinato, drone, simple part-singing)	2. Enjoy making, changing and combining sounds; experiment with different ways of producing sounds with voice, musical instruments, simple music technology, body sounds
3. Begin to recognise and musically demonstrate awareness of a link between shape and pitch using graphic notations	3. Begin to recognise and musically demonstrate awareness of a link between shape and pitch using graphic notations
4. Create simple accompaniments	4. Create simple rhythmic patterns
5. Communicate ideas, thoughts and feelings through simple musical demonstration, language, movement and other art forms, giving simple justifications of reasons for responses	5. Demonstrate understanding of the differences between pulse and rhythm, e.g. through physical movement, playing, singing and/or discussion

Example Statements Stage A	Example Statements Stage B	Example Statements Stage C	Example Statements Stage D
1. Enjoy singing, playing, trying out and changing sounds, explore sounds and music through play.	1. Enjoy making, playing, changing and combining sounds, experiment with different ways of producing sounds with voice, musical instruments, simple music technology, 'body sounds' (tapping, clicking, marching, stamping etc.).	1. Use voice, sounds, technology and instruments in creative ways.	1. Experiment with voice, sounds, technology and instruments in creative ways and to explore new techniques.
2. Recognise and broadly control changes in timbre, tempo, pitch and dynamics when playing instruments and vocally.	2. Sing in tune within a limited pitch range and perform with a good sense of pulse and rhythm.	2. Sing and play confidently and fluently, maintaining an appropriate pulse.	2. Maintain a strong sense of pulse and recognise and self-correct when going out of time.
3. Sing broadly in tune within a limited pitch range.	3. Join in and stop as appropriate.	3. Suggest, follow and lead simple performance directions.	3. Demonstrate increasing confidence, expression, skill and level of musicality through taking different roles in performance and rehearsal.
4. Follow and offer simple musical instructions and actions.	4. Follow and lead simple performance directions, demonstrating understanding of these through movement, singing and playing (including, but not limited to, dynamics and tempo, starting and stopping, adhering to 'starts and stops' i.e. sound and silence). Pupils could suggest and try out their own ideas.	4. Sing within an appropriate vocal range with clear diction, mostly accurate tuning, control of breathing and appropriate tone.	4. Lead an independent part in a group when singing or playing (e.g. rhythm, ostinato, drone, simple part singing, etc.).
5. Keep a steady pulse with some accuracy, e.g. through tapping, clapping, marching, playing (develop 'internalising' skills).	5. Listen with increased concentration, responding appropriately to a variety of live and recorded music, making statements and observations about the music and through movement, sound-based and other creative responses.	5. Demonstrate musical quality – e.g. clear starts, ends of pieces / phrases, technical accuracy etc.	5. Use a variety of musical devices, timbres, textures, techniques etc. when creating and making music.
6. Listen to ideas from others, taking turns as appropriate to the context, e.g. passing around instruments, sharing, listening to others playing/singing/ sharing ideas	6. Respond to musical cues.	6. Maintain an independent part in a small group when playing or singing (e.g. rhythm, ostinato, drone, simple part singing etc.).	6. Create music which demonstrates understanding of structure and discuss the choices made.

Example Statements Stage A	Example Statements Stage B	Example Statements Stage C	Example Statements Stage D
7. Show awareness of the audience when performing	7. Musically demonstrate increased understanding and use of basic musical features as appropriate related to a specific music context (e.g. graduation of sound – getting louder, softer, higher, lower, faster, slower, describe the quality of sounds and how they are made, combined etc. and names of common classroom instruments), supported by verbal explanation, pictures, movements etc. as appropriate.	7. Create simple rhythmic patterns, melodies and accompaniments.	7. Listen and evaluate a range of live and recorded music from different traditions, genres, styles and times, responding appropriately to the context. Share opinions about own and others' music and be willing to justify these.
8. Create music, and suggest symbols to represent sounds (e.g. a large foot for the daddy bear, small foot for baby bear).	8. Begin to recognise and musically demonstrate awareness of a link between shape and pitch using graphic notations.	8. Communicate ideas, thoughts and feelings through simple musical demonstration, language, movement and other art forms, giving simple justifications of reasons for responses.	8. Be perceptive to music and communicate personal thoughts and feelings, through discussion, movement, sound-based and other creative responses such as visual arts.
9. Make physical movements that represent sounds (e.g. move like a snake, an elephant, grow like a tree in response to music).	9. Begin to recognise rhythmic patterns found in speech, e.g. saying / chanting names, counting syllables in names etc.	9. Offer comments about own and others' work and ways to improve; accept feedback and suggestions from others.	9. Critique own and others' work, offering specific comments and justifying these.
10. Comment on and respond to recordings of own voice, other classroom sounds, musical instruments etc.	10. Demonstrate understanding of the differences between pulse and rhythm through physical movement, playing, singing.	10. Aurally identify, recognise, respond to and use musically (as appropriate) basic symbols (standard and invented), including rhythms from standard Western notation (e.g. crotchets, quavers) and basic changes in pitch within a limited range.	10. As appropriate, follow basic shapes of music (including staff and other notations) through singing and playing short passages of music when working as a musician.

Figure 8.1 Exemplar criterion statements for primary music (adapted from Daubney and Fautley, 2014)

Assessment across a unit of work

Unit assessment should be directly related to the learning sought within the unit. For example, a Year 5 unit on 'songs and chants for sporting fixtures' might focus on the learning objectives in Table 8.2.

From these learning objectives, the unit can be planned and assessment criteria defined. Assessment criteria for one group of pupils might include the following:

- Sing with good tone, tuning, diction and awareness of blending voice with others.
- Hold a vocal line as part of a group when singing simple harmony parts for part of a song.
- Aurally identify scale passages and show accurately the broad direction of pitch movement (i.e. ascending or descending).
- Confidently improvise vocal chants in a small group.
- Share ideas about how the music makes you feel and offer suggestions as to why.

To document these criteria as they emerge, you might do something as simple as drawing triangles next to a list of the learning sought (Table 8.3). An advantage to a system such as this is that it is quick and easy to update as you observe pupils throughout their work. Fixed assessment points in a lesson are not required and you just need to make mental notes for yourself as you see the learning unfolding. It also provides a very quick way to scan your notes in order to further personalise learning which helps to provide appropriate support and challenge for all. If audio/video is integral to the learning process, it is relatively straightforward to capture 'evidence' of musical behaviours. This is discussed further later in this chapter.

Table 8.2   Examples of learning objectives for a unit of work

Singing	<ul><li>develop accurate timing, pitch and a good singing tone</li><li>develop experience of being part of a group when singing simple harmony parts</li><li>develop awareness of the blending of voices when singing with others and develop their own contribution to this as part of the class ensemble</li></ul>
Creating music	<ul><li>improvise short rhythmical chants suitable for sporting fixtures</li><li>contribute ideas to the production of a 'class song' with a chorus, verses and simple instrumental accompaniments</li></ul>
Critical engagement	<ul><li>respond to a range of live and recorded music through art, movement, music and discussion</li><li>express how the music makes them think and feel, providing reasons for their responses and being responsive to others' comments and suggestions</li><li>aurally recognise scale passages when singing, playing and listening and be able to physically show the direction of the pitch movement</li></ul>

Table 8.3 Documenting musical learning

	Sing with good tone, tuning, diction and awareness of blending voice with others	Hold a vocal line as part of a group when singing simple harmony parts for part of a song	Identify scale passages and show accurately the broad movement of direction	Confidently improvise vocal chants in a small group	Share ideas about how the music makes you feel and why
Lizzy	▲	▲	▲	▲	▲
Gary	△	▲	∧	∧	∧
Ed	∧	∧	△	∧	▲
Lydia	▲	▲	△	▲	▲

∧ = working towards
△ = working at
▲ = exceeding

From the results recorded in Table 8.3, the teacher will instantly be able to see that Lizzy needs a greater degree of challenge in the next unit of work as she is easily exceeding the teacher's current expectations.

Learning criteria: To share or not to share ... that is the question!

Sometimes, but not always, you may want to discuss or develop the 'success criteria' with pupils. For example, when creating a song for a sporting occasion, as in the above example, it is useful to think about the audience, the purpose and the structure of songs used for this occasion (for example, listening to, singing or playing examples and creating the structure from different coloured Lego bricks in order to establish that there is a recurring chorus, verses, an introduction, possibly another section – a middle 8 or an instrumental, and to think about how it ends). It may be useful to further break this down so that children recognise that the chorus is probably catchy and memorable and might have a particular rhyming structure. Therefore, working together with the class, the 'success criteria' become co-constructed and have a purpose. This is non-threatening to individuals and to the class, and builds ownership.

At other times, it is unnecessary to discuss the learning outcomes or success criteria in advance, and is better to just let the learning emerge. For example, when giving children opportunities to improvise the sounds of different shades of purple on a Kandinsky painting, giving them success criteria and over-modelling or discussing this in advance is likely to shut down the creative exploration and risk-taking as children start to be inhibited by trying to seek the 'right' answer.

How do you assess?

Identifying what you are assessing and why helps establish the best way(s) to assess. The most useful assessment for children is formative, developmental assessment.

Wiliam (2009: 12) refers to this kind of assessment as: 'feedback that moves the learning forward ... the major purpose of feedback is to provide the learner with guidance on what to do next, rather than telling her or him about what was deficient in the last piece of work.'

Great teachers always have their 'radar' up in the classroom – scanning, watching, listening and thinking; working out if and when to intervene and how to do this.

TASK 8.2

Consider the following scenarios and identify strategies that you think are productive and those which are detrimental to musical learning/ownership.

Diego, Jeff and George are working together to create a melody to go with a repeated chordal accompaniment recorded on a backing track (C, A minor, F and G) using tuned percussion instruments. Five minutes before the end of the lesson, Mr Bromley, the teacher, wanders over to the group.

Scenario A

Mr Bromley [stops the group]: 'OK, boys, show me what you've got.' The boys start up the backing track and start to play along. After 10 bars of music, they grind to a halt and the backing track continues. Mr Bromley stops the track and then says: 'Well done! I particularly liked the lyrical quality of the melody as it moved step-wise – the notes were all near each other. How do you think you might be able to continue from here'? The boys chip in various suggestions about making the melody longer. Mr Bromley asks about the notes of the chords used in the backing track and how these might be useful. George suggests adding a simple harmony part based on the root notes of the repeating chord pattern. Mr Bromley asks what the boys will do with their next 5 minutes, listens to their ideas, smiles encouragingly and walks away.

Scenario B

Mr Bromley [stops the group]: 'Some of it is great but you seem to have run out of material and just stop abruptly. You need to develop the melody further; just finish it off so that it finishes back on the root note of "C" [picks up the beaters and plays the ending] and perhaps just follow the chords so where it changes to A minor add an A, where it goes to F play the F notes, and so on and so forth. I'll be back in 5 minutes to listen to it again.'

In scenario A, Mr Bromley provides positive encouragement and specific feedback about what he liked and he justifies this. Through careful questioning, he elicits responses from the boys about their next steps and how they will do this. He gives a specific time instruction (5 minutes) and leaves the ownership of the piece and the creative choices with the boys, guiding this only through conversation.

However, in scenario B, the comments are much more 'top-down'. Mr Bromley dwells on what is deficient, risks taking ownership away from the boys and gives specific suggestions (verbally and musically modelling) in order to make the piece 'right'. The positive part of the conversation – 'Some of it is great' – is so unspecific that the boys are unclear about which section Mr Bromley is referring to.

We can glean from these scenarios that feedback needs to be specific, and that the way in which we intervene and direct conversations and musical learning is also very important. In a study of 20 teachers in secondary school who were teaching composing, it was noted that 19 gave specific verbal instructions about how to improve, and 15 also played musical examples of what should happen (Daubney, 2008). Time implications, such as the lesson finishing soon, meant that teachers often hurried to get to a 'finished product' at all cost, with little regard for the process or creative exploration of pupils' ideas. Clearly, this has a significant impact on ownership, can affect motivation and leaves children wondering what the purpose was, if not to find the 'solution' that the teacher was looking for. Such strategies are not always appreciated; this quote from a pupil on a creative arts project discusses one teenager's views on working with a visiting artist:

> She was really nice and really helpful, but they, like, let you do it yourself. They showed you ideas, but then they wouldn't just do it all for you, which is generally what teachers do. When you were stuck, you could ask her for some ideas, but she wouldn't say, 'I think you should do this'; she walked away and let us discuss the ideas with our group leader. (Daubney, 2007: 40)

This supports Hargreaves' (2013: 230) assertion that: 'It becomes important to find out from the children themselves how their interpretation and use of teachers' feedback relates to their sense of autonomy.'

Getting children involved in assessment

> Without the learner's perspective, the crucially important affective and interactional aspects of learners' responses to feedback are likely to be missing. (Hargreaves, 2013: 230)

Even without being prompted, it is likely that many children already self-assess their own musical activities and pass judgements on others' music. Rehearsing music to make improvements requires a high degree of critical listening and self-assessment in order to continually make small adjustments and critique effectiveness. When creating music, critical judgement helps us to decide whether or not a particular section is fine, needs removing or adapting. Therefore, this monitoring and the constant cyclic revision process are integral to assessing and linked to metacognition (discussed in Chapter 2).

There are many ways in which children get actively involved in assessment. This does not rely on 'judging' final products against a pre-defined set of criteria; by then, the opportunities for learning and development through the process, which is where most of the 'gains' will come, will have passed. Simple strategies such as showing thumbs up, sideways or down, or traffic lights (red, amber and green), can be a very quick way for a teacher to gain perspective on how pupils feel and then adjust the learning pathway as necessary (although asking pupils to close their eyes is also useful so that they are not feeling pressured to give a certain response that will be seen or judged by other children). Activities such as mind maps (e.g. 'tell me everything you know about African music' at the start of a unit) are great for finding out what pupils are familiar with already and also to highlight misconceptions.

There are many opportunities to engage with children during the musical process – by listening in and guiding their conversations if necessary, through careful questioning, through asking them to provide comments on successful aspects of work and specific ideas for improvement or future development. Think about this example:

> Year 5 has learnt the opening section of a rap about the Tropic of Capricorn and identified the countries it crosses. Flossy, Bernard and Douglas have developed a mind map of their ideas about what it is like in Australia and compiled a short 4-line rap. Mr Duncan, the music teacher, observes that they have gone off task and wanders over. He asks the group to perform what they have so far. At the end of the short performance, he asks some questions about the work in progress, particularly about the rhyming structure and the length of the lines. Together, they think about words to rhyme and comple- ment the line 'Australia is always hot, you'd love to come Down Under'. Mr Duncan's focus is completely on the development of the lyrics, not on the performance of it. He asks about their strategy for development and Flossy tells him they will look for rhyming couplets and count the syllables in each line. With a nod and a smile, Mr Duncan says they will have 5 more minutes to work on their section and wanders away to listen to another group.

Creating a supportive environment takes time but it is critical if you want children to feel confident enough to share their work with each other and to give and accept constructive feedback. There are many ways in which this could be embedded in the classroom. Some examples are included in Table 8.4.

Table 8.4 Examples of strategies to get children involved in assessment

Possible strategy	Example	Why useful – example
Group feedback	As a 'mini plenary' during a lesson where children are working in pairs on computers to compose their own piece, share the work in progress with another pair and ask them to identify one thing they thought was successful about the piece so far (giving a reason), and offering two ideas for development in the next part of the process	Lots of ideas shared with a small group, filtered and refined before feedback is given. Focus is on what went well and on providing specific ideas for development

Possible strategy	Example	Why useful – example
Planning time	At the beginning of a task, or after feedback, before pupils go off to rehearse or develop their work, they are given 3 minutes of planning time without the instruments in which to plan what they are going to do	This could be enhanced with a previous 'work in progress' recording. This technique encourages pupils to develop a plan for what they are going to do and also potentially set some specific target areas for development
Exemplar work	Listen to a recording of work in progress from another class. If you were in the audience, what do you think about their singing? Using the card that you have been given (e.g. tuning, pronunciation), comment on what you hear and give specific advice for improvement	This task encourages pupils to think about developing quality and directs their attention when listening. Pupils take ideas on their own work in a non-threatening way. The marking is anonymous so it removes the personal aspects of comments and the potential peer pressure of friendships
'Expert' panel	Those pupils whose work is being showcased sit at the front of the room and answer questions about it, which are generated by the rest of the class (small group discussion first is usually a good strategy to get the questions going)	This allows everyone to be involved. It also encourages the audience to ask questions rather than give comments, and gives pupils on show the opportunity to think through what is being asked, respond and find ways forward. The teacher may wish to make brief notes on a card to give to the group at the end of the panel
Parents' evening	Children choose work they want to share and present the audio/video to their parents, explaining what they did and anything else they want to say about it	Sharing with an external audience, needing to be selective and engaging with a 'back catalogue' of work

One of the most effective ways for children from Year 5 onwards to be involved in assessment is through creating and updating a *personal profile* on polar graph paper, as you were encouraged to do in Task 1.4. You could ask a question such as 'what makes a great singer?' (see Figure 8.2), then ask pupils to identify key attributes (and then the opposites) and then rate themselves against these. This is an activity children really enjoy and it leads to some enlightening findings and a wide range of ideas. For example, in relation to singing, many children note factors relating to stage presence, communicating expressively with an audience, and also the importance of movement. They are also well aware of many of the technical aspects of singing. The emergent conversations are really interesting as children are often very clear why they are a '4 out of 10' and what they will need to do to get to 5 (i.e. target setting).

It is also interesting to think about how you, as their teacher, would have rated them against each of the attributes they individually chose, as the discrepancies can sometimes show a child's under-confidence and, at other times, you may find out

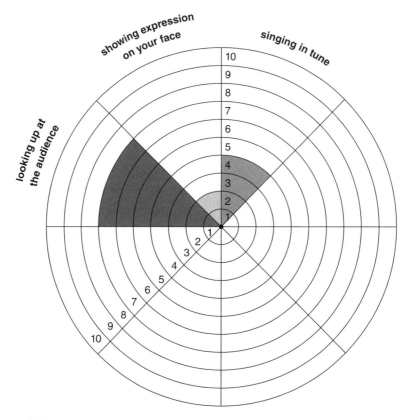

Figure 8.2 Example personal construct chart – what are the attributes of a great singer?

something you didn't know about them, particularly relating to their music life outside school. Expect the unexpected with this exercise – children are astute and able to communicate sophisticated ideas showing far greater depth of understanding than would be elicited if the teacher were to provide the constructs. You can come back to this a few months later and see how much their ideas and ratings have changed. Remember that, as we become more enlightened and experienced, our ideas about what constitutes a particular number might be modified. The discussion, target setting and future actions are the most important parts of this strategy.

The role of dialogue and questioning

Many effective formative assessment strategies in music education relate to dialogue, discussion and questioning; these aim to develop reflective thinking and future actions. Questions are a great way to nurture curiosity, imagination and creativity, and children should be encouraged to ask questions. Perhaps some teachers stay away from encouraging children to ask too many questions, in case they are unable to give a satisfactory response themselves. It is OK not to know the answer to a question. The teacher does not need to pretend to be an expert on everything and often there are 30 other eager voices in the classroom waiting to be heard! If you are asked a question you don't know the answer to, you could throw this open to the class and also acknowledge that it is a very good question that you can all go away and research and discuss again tomorrow.

Questions that children generate themselves are often very interesting. Take this example:

> Year 6 is listening to an extract of the song *Radio Ga Ga* by Queen. At the end of the 30-second extract, Mrs Machin stops the recording and gives each child an A4 piece of paper. She introduces the task, which aims to generate interesting questions about the music to ask other people. Everyone should write down a question next to the top pre-printed stem word – 'what'. Mrs Machin provides two examples – 'what was the first word sung in this song'? 'What images does the music bring to your mind when you listen to it'? Once the question has been written, the top of the paper should be folded over so that the word 'how' is showing. Pass the paper on to the next person in a clockwise direction. Then repeat with each word until all six stems – what, explain, show, compare, how and why – have been completed and the papers moved on one last time so that everyone has a completely new set of questions. After checking that the class understands, Mrs Machin switches on the recording of the song and the questions are generated. At the end, each child reads out the most interesting question on their paper and they discuss responses to these in small groups.

Through gaining insight into what the children are thinking about and focusing on, the teacher can guide their attention, encourage their discussions and plan the next steps. Often, the questions the children generate are far more interesting and probing than those asked by a teacher, and an activity such as this gives pupils ownership of the questions.

Age-defined criteria?

In some subjects, there is currently an unhealthy obsession with age-related norms – in other words, 'at the age of 9, a child should be able to do, know and understand x, y and z'. Thankfully, there are no such statutory criteria or expectations for primary music in England and neither should there be – children are not robots. They have different experiences, different rates of learning and many other factors that influence how, when and where their musical learning journey develops. Age-defined criteria assume uniform, linear progression and are nonsense in terms of musical learning (and learning in general). Nevertheless, there may be a set of age-related criteria that your school uses from a published scheme or that the music coordinator is expected to develop. You should however treat such frameworks with extreme caution; imagine you are a 9-year-old child who loves music, only to be told that against an 'age-related set of statements' you are below average. The immediate and long-term impact of this is likely to be devastating.

Developing a digital portfolio

In art, you have the artefacts, photographs and physical examples of work created; in English, you have the stories and the writing; and in maths, there are exercise books. In music though, once the time has passed, there is nothing left but memories. Making audio and video recordings is a very powerful part of a musical process, helping work to develop over time. It is also a very effective and compelling way to show progress over time, and to make the process of learning at least equally as important as the product.

Ofsted (2012: 38) notes the following:

> The most effective assessment practice observed helped students to listen more accurately to their own work, helped them identify for themselves where improvements were needed, and showed them how to improve through expert musical modelling by the teacher. However, too many schools did not assess in this way, or exploit the use of audio and video recordings in the classroom to listen to and assess students' work more accurately. **A well-ordered catalogue of recordings over time, supported by commentaries and scores, provides a very effective and compelling way to demonstrate students' musical progress**.

From this, it is critical to note that audio and video are very powerful tools, but their impact is lost when they are used only to mark 'end of unit recordings' and are effectively stuck in a drawer or converted to numbers on a spreadsheet as 'evidence', in case anyone asks. With the explosion of mobile technology in recent years, it is quick and easy to capture, store and share recordings. As in the early years settings described earlier, there are some very good digital portfolio packages; alternatively, recordings could be uploaded to cloud storage, or you may even use one of a number of commercial applications (apps) for this purpose. Many schools are concerned with video or photographic material being uploaded to an open website (mostly due to child protection issues), so having an internal system gets around this and also encourages 'work in progress' to be captured and used effectively.

There are also some excellent examples of schools developing websites or blogs where work is uploaded, often in audio form and able to be commented on (although the teacher is the gatekeeper to publishing comments). This developing forum is itself a 'well-ordered catalogue of recordings over time', providing a great way for your pupils to authentically share their work with others and to hear their own progress over time. The majority of work pupils undertake in music will be in groups varying in size and structure. There should be no expectation that each pupil will have individual recordings of their work – this would be unwieldy to manage and is not representative of classroom learning situations. Having a bank of recordings to go back to as the main component in a digital portfolio, as described above, is possibly the only genuinely musical way to show progress over time.

Chapter summary

Assessment is fundamental to teaching and learning in music. The breadth of the term needs to be better understood, along with recognition of the many ways in which assessment can nurture or destroy children and their learning. Formative, developmental assessment is most important for teachers and pupils; as Swanwick (1997: 205) reminds us, 'all teaching involves responding appropriately to what students do and say'. Music teachers should avoid sharing numbers, grades and other methods by which children compare themselves with each other.

In Chapter 1, you were encouraged to consider your values in relation to music education. There are three interlinking questions that you should seek to answer honestly at regular intervals. The first relates to your values. In assessing the effectiveness of the music education you are leading, are the values you want underpinned by your curriculum and behaviours? In other words, do you *assess your values*? Do you *value what and how you assess*? If the answer to either of these questions is no, you need to do some work to redress this.

The second question relates directly to your pupils and their experiences. By placing yourself mentally in the seat of three different pupils at the end of every lesson and answering the question 'what did they get from my lesson today?', you can get an idea of the effectiveness of your lesson and a good basis to realistically reflect on. Of course, asking the children what they think is even more important, as you may be completely misjudging what they would say!

Just as the curriculum sends messages to pupils about what music is and who it is for, so does your use of assessment. The third question to answer, therefore, is 'what message does your use of assessment send about music education?' Is it the message you want to come through? Does it underpin your values? It is certainly something to keep striving towards and developing throughout your career and absolutely key to providing a musically inspiring education.

Great assessment in music is not like that in, say, maths, English or science. We need to push against any movement to impose unrealistic and damaging one-size-fits-all approaches and remember the uniqueness of the subject and the power of high quality, intuitive and informative musical assessment that serves the purpose of promoting musical learning and engagement.

Further reading

Fautley, M. (2010) *Assessment in Music Education*. Oxford: Oxford University Press.

Fautley, M. and Daubney, A. (2014) A Guide to Curriculum, Assessment and Progression. Webinar, 16 July. Incorporated Society of Musicians (ISM)/Birmingham City University. Available at: http://docplayer.net/14439352-Assessment-and-progression-webinar-presented-by-professor-martin-fautley-dr-alison-daubney-wednesday-16-th-july-2014.html

Swann, M., Peacock, A., Hart, S. and Drummond, M.J. (2012) *Creating Learning Without Limits*. Maidenhead: Open University Press.

9

MUSIC: THE HEARTBEAT OF THE SCHOOL AND CURRICULUM

> Like any other school we're under pressure to deliver the results on the core subjects, but the creative arts are the key to unlocking the love of learning that we take very seriously. (Sue Bundy, deputy head teacher at Loughton Primary School, Milton Keynes, in Daubney et al., 2014: 28)

Introduction

Music is powerful. There is absolutely no doubt about its potential to draw children into learning, permeating the cultural fabric of every school. We must recognise and acknowledge how important music is to children's lives and build on this, rather than ignoring it.

There is substantive empirical evidence about the power of music to help children develop all kinds of skills – for example, learning to read, developing fine and gross motor skills, developing memory and language, developing recall skills (Hallam, 2015), given a specific and defined set of conditions. Equally, there is compelling evidence that musical learning helps children to concentrate, to feel good about themselves and to work with others.

This chapter explores some of the ways in which music can be embedded through the curriculum and more widely across primary schools.

Objectives

Through this chapter you will:

- explore the possibilities for using music to access the wider school curriculum
- identify specific examples of how and where this might happen
- establish ways in which music can be introduced into other aspects of school life, e.g. assembly, extra-curricular activities, around the school and to punctuate routines in the school day.

Learning *in*, *through* and *about* music

Clearly, music is a subject in its own right, with its own processes, goals and language. In life, however, music does not predominantly exist in isolation; it is entwined with films, dance, soundtracks, adverts, music videos, theatre, rituals and so much more. Successful music education establishes the music in our bones through deep and contextually rich engagement with music. Learning *in* music means thinking and acting musically; immersing ourselves in authentic musical practices – playing and creating music, being curious and playful, meddling with sounds for the enjoyment of doing so, engaging as a critical musician and auditor and being open to a myriad of musical experiences, influences and situations. The first overarching message of this book is that a rich education *in* music throughout a child's early years and primary schooling is crucial for instilling in them a lifelong love of music.

Learning *about* music is integral to learning in music – we learn about music through being engaged *in* music. From a teacher's perspective, there are always things to learn *about* music – for example, where particular music comes from, how many beats are in a bar on a particular piece, the key signatures of a passage of music, how music makes us feel and why it does so. Yet, these are things that only really make sense within the context of experiencing and feeling them. For example, it is much easier to recognise that some music has three beats in a bar once we have waltzed around the room with our friends and experienced this for ourselves.

At other times, music is the vehicle through which children learn something related to another subject or skill. Learning *through* music can be an extremely powerful way of helping children access learning in different curriculum areas. For some teachers, this is how they feel most confident to begin to introduce music into their classrooms, which is fine as we all need to start somewhere. To be clear, this is not necessarily music education – using music in this way does not automatically seek to develop the specific musical knowledge, skills, understanding, thoughts and feelings that an immersive musical experience would and is not a substitute for dedicated musical learning. Yet, given children's interest in music, it is perfectly positioned to take an important role across learning.

Models of music within the curriculum

The place of music in the curriculum depends on how the curriculum is organised. Here are some possibilities:

1. The Creative Curriculum – also called 'Learning Journeys' or 'Topic-based'. In this model, learning across curriculum subjects is related to a topic/theme – this could be a book, historical period, geographical feature, etc., in which they are immersed for a set period of time (e.g. half a term). The timetable may be quite flexible so that the days are quite free flowing and all subjects are covered within the school week but not at specific times.
2. As above with a topic/theme but specific subjects have a set time in the school timetable – for example, the class has a music lesson between 1.30 and 2.30 every Wednesday afternoon.
3. Music is taught as a separate subject with its own units of work unrelated to a more generic topic/theme.

The delivery of music also varies. For example, music in each class is taught by:

(a) the class teacher as a regularly timetabled lesson
(b) the class teacher but does not have a specific 'slot' on the timetable
(c) another member of school staff who is a music specialist/subject coordinator
(d) another member of school staff who is not a music specialist/subject coordinator
(e) a visiting music specialist delivering the curriculum throughout the year
(f) a visiting whole-class instrumental teacher who delivers a specific project or programme for a fixed, short-term period of time.

TASK 9.1

Identify which of the above apply to your own class. Multiple combinations of these may be present and there may also be other models which are not listed.

Even if you are not expected to teach music at this point in time, it is beneficial to immerse yourself in the experience of teaching music through observing and co-teaching. There is a high chance that you will need to teach music at some point in the future, so gaining some confidence, skills and experience now will be helpful. It will also help you experiment with ways that you can use music across the curriculum to enhance other areas of learning.

Models of cross-curricular learning

Barnes (2012: 137) notes that: 'Music is possibly the second most universally recognized discipline after language.' There are endless possibilities for music to permeate the curriculum and wider school culture, making learning exciting and accessible, inspiring children to explore and learn in inventive ways.

Barnes' substantive research on cross-curricular learning led to the development of a series of models highlighting the relationships between different subjects and experiences. The ideas in this chapter explore potential roles and the place of music through the lens of Barnes' (2012, 2015) models of cross-curricular teaching and learning, specifically 'tokenistic', 'hierarchical', 'multi-disciplinary', 'interdisciplinary', 'opportunistic' and 'double-focused'.

Tokenistic learning

As the name suggests, tokenistic learning is just that – an exercise which is for the sake of it and does not add any obvious value to learning and, as Barnes suggests, should not really be considered to be cross-curricular. In terms of music, this might include singing, playing or listening to something related to a theme or topic but without any obvious planned or expected learning or development of skills or knowledge – for example, singing 'head, shoulders, knees and toes' at the start of a biology lesson.

Hierarchical learning

In 'hierarchical learning', a subject is used as a vehicle to enhance learning in another subject, for example using singing to learn times tables, to practise or identify phonics sounds, to help learn the names of different parts of the body or to understand rhyming couplets in poetry. Barnes (2012: 140) describes hierarchical learning as 'playing the handmaiden's role, humbly serving a more important subject'. Music often occupies this 'supporting' role. Conversely though, music, and in particular, songs and singing, are very powerful in supporting communication, motivation and enjoyment, developing or consolidating learning in another subject:

> In a phonics lesson, Year 2 was concentrating on the consonant diagraph 'sh'. Groups of six children were given a short poem or saying to recite to the others in the class, and they rehearsed these with the support of the teaching assistant and the teacher. The first group stood up to perform the phrase 'she sells sea shells on the seashore'. The rest of the class listened diligently and bashed the boomwhacker on the floor every time the 'sh' sound was heard. The children repeated the phrase all together. The second group then performed its excerpt, and again the class listened intently for the 'sh' sounds with boomwhackers at the ready:
>
> 'I washed and brushed my shiny hair
>
> And shook my head to dry it'.
>
> As the process continued, Mr Biddle extracted the recognition from the class that the 'sh' sound was not always at the beginning of the word and the class began to create lists of words where 'sh' appeared at different points – the beginning, middle and end, and where 'sh' sounds in words had other spellings such as ocean.

As a music teacher, it is not uncommon to be asked to 'teach the children a song on the Romans' or another topic. In some schools, I would go so far as to say that this is viewed as musical learning and is the sum total of music education. To be clear, I rarely consider this to be the case unless the focus of the learning is to develop something related either to the quality of the music or musical experience, or to develop specific musical skills or musical understanding; and not just singing through a song for the sake of it. This is not to diminish the experience; I personally only know the days of the week in French because we sang a song about it at secondary school, although it was only years later that I realised the second line of the song was 'and the week begins again' – the word 'week' may have been useful to know!

TASK 9.2

Think about a lesson you are planning for another subject. Identify a specific opportunity for music to enhance this learning and plan for music to be a part of the activities in the lesson. Be very clear about your learning objective and how some kind of engagement with music will support this.

It doesn't always have to be the case that music is the subservient subject in a hierarchical cross-curricular relationship. It could be that there is a defined musical learning focus that can be supported in other ways – for example, practising tongue twisters to make the diction clearer; using drama to create an atmosphere which helps children to understand the oppressive context, mood and feeling of specific music representing the war; rolling tennis balls in pairs to help to feel and keep a steady beat.

TASK 9.3

Think about the learning objectives planned for your next music lesson. Consider whether and how another subject area may be able to support this learning.

Multi-disciplinary learning

In some cases, the learning model may initially seem to be hierarchical, yet the focus could be very slightly shifted in order for the learning to become multi-disciplinary. All included subjects are important in 'multi-disciplinary' learning. According to Barnes (2012: 141), 'several subjects are called on separately to bring understanding to a theme, experience or idea ... [creating] powerful and emotionally significant experiences for the children and teachers', and, through this, enabling learning in all subjects.

Many localities organise massed singing events; these have the potential to be powerful multi-disciplinary learning experiences. For example, the 2014 annual primary schools Christmas concert in Brighton included songs written by children from local special schools, crafted by animateur James Redwood. The lyrics and narration were based around the theme of Christmas in the trenches, and the concert took place 100 years after the start of the First World War; 1,400 children sang and Makaton signed the songs, with aspects of the storytelling contributed by pupils from special schools using BIGMack switches. Many children had studied aspects of the First World War through historical accounts, poetry and literacy. Crafting, learning and performing the songs contributed to pupils' 'powerful and emotionally significant experiences', advancing their understanding of songs as evocative ways to communicate stories, and developing their singing and signing skills in a multitude of ways. The focus on the quality of the singing and the ensemble skills for the performance, as well as the contextual understanding which it helped to develop, meant that music went beyond the simple 'handmaiden's role'.

Interdisciplinary learning

Barnes (2012: 144) describes interdisciplinary learning as 'creatively combining the approaches of two or more subjects ... subjects are not just applied to a single experience, theme or event but are combined in response to that experience', leading to increased understanding in each subject. There are many possibilities for incorporating music in this way.

Between 2013 and 2014, the English Folk Dance and Song Society (EFDSS) led 'The Full English', a programme of work with 19 projects in primary and secondary schools highlighting the power of folk arts, heritage and songs. Projects utilised local folk materials as starting points for wonderful cross-curricular learning spanning the curriculum. It also flipped the idea of songs 'supporting' other subjects on its head, as the initial cross-curricular stimuli materials were the songs themselves.

Marton Primary School in Lincolnshire really took this idea to heart and threaded fabulous cross-curricular work across the primary curriculum for Years 3 to 6 for the duration of a school term. 'Made in Marton' was an immersive experience for pupils, teachers and the local community. The project introduced traditional music, songs, dances and folklore from Lincolnshire as a springboard to exploration of the social history and heritage of Marton. Folk materials were used as a stimulus in art, literacy and geography, and the local environment was explored, leading to the creation of a permanent signposted heritage walk around the village. For some children, a visit to the Museum of Lincolnshire Life was their first trip to the local city. The children also worked with people of all ages from their village to develop a community band, another lasting impact of the work. Ben Stevenson, Marton's head teacher, said of the project:

> I hoped The Full English would be a way of bringing local history alive in a relevant and purposeful way, but it surpassed my expectations. It reached across the curriculum. It improved the standard of imaginative writing. It prompted us to start a community band. And it definitely deepened the children's love of history ... They could see themselves as a link in a chain that stretches back generations. That has given them another strand in their sense of identity and a renewed respect for the community. (Daubney et al., 2014: 8)

'Made in Marton' had multiple strands and produced much work which the children were proud of. All this started from local links – music, stories (Dick Turpin apparently stayed at the local pub), dances, locations and traditions. Yet, through the folk arts, tangible and intangible cultural heritage were brought together and developed in imaginative ways – new songs and stories emerged and things previously not crossing the children's radar were explored, considered and developed. Music was not a bolt-on, but instead stimulated a great deal of high quality, in-depth work and deep learning. As in the example of multidisciplinary learning, the experiences were authentic and there was shared recognition of their worth. External validation came from sharing and celebrating work produced in the classroom, from playing at a barn dance and from concerts and performances in and out of school.

Teachers were excited by the way songs enriched the curriculum and acted as the springboard to deep inter-disciplinary and creative cross-curricular learning experiences. The music created the bridge to cultures, times and places. Songs have exciting syntax and language – they tell stories, introduce characters, evoke images and feelings, and so much more. In essence, they are perfectly placed to be firmly at the centre of high quality inter-disciplinary experiences bringing the curriculum to life.

Opportunistic learning

Barnes (2012: 146) describes opportunistic learning as 'child-led, unpredictable and including an element of risk'. Music has considerable potential here too, particularly when bringing in children's own musical ideas and influences. Children sing and hum frequently – in the playground, in assembly, and even when rehearsing and choreographing their latest favourite pop songs. There is a significant amount a teacher could do with these opportunistic events – ranging from 30-second interludes and transitions in a lesson, through taking children's ideas and helping them develop those ideas in ways which give them ownership and control, to using these as the centre of the learning experience. Here is an example from the classroom:

> At the end of Friday lunchtime, Mrs Shaw's Year 5 class came in from break in a sombre mood, having been told off by the midday meals supervisor for arguing with each other and fighting in the playground. Mrs Shaw took the register and the children read their chosen books in silence for 10 minutes. At the end of this time, Mrs Shaw gave each pupil a Post-it note and instructed them to write or draw a message about hope and friendship to someone they cared about. A 2-minute countdown timer was set on the board and the children got to work with a sense of urgency. At the end of this time, they were invited to share their messages with the rest of the pupils on their table.

> Moving the tables out of the way and indicating to pupils to place their chairs in a circle, a karaoke version of the song *Count on Me* by Bruno Mars was displayed on the whiteboard; this was the song pupils had come into the classroom singing that morning after the junior school assembly. Mrs Shaw started singing along with the song and the class joined in; the mood in the classroom continued to lift and the children grinned and swayed to the 'oohs', making eye contact with each other. This moved into a circle-time activity which involved discussing the events of lunchtime and pupils' thoughts and feelings.

Count on Me is essentially a song about friendship, linking with schools' spiritual, moral, social and cultural (SMSC) agenda, and in this case it was brought into circle time and developed with the whole class. Flexible teachers often follow pupils' ideas, going off on tangents but also making explicit links; there are many possibilities for taking pupils' music and musical ideas into other lessons and parts of the school and making these integral to the learning and wider classroom experience. Early years teachers are often masters at this, yet there remains much untapped potential across all primary school learning.

Double-focus learning

Barnes (2012: 148) describes this as treating a subject 'firstly as a separate discipline with its own rules, language and knowledge and second, in combination with other subjects'.

An example of a double focus on music and literacy is given below:

Year 6 pupils were developing their creative writing skills, thinking about how powerful language and rich description evoked a particular setting and mood. In music lessons, they were exploring 'programme music', using examples of Mussorgsky's *Pictures at an Exhibition* to set words, create music and explore relationships between visual arts and music.

Bringing these two together, Miss Raggl introduced an activity to help use music to generate images and language. Four Post-it notes were given to each pupil. Playing the first of three excerpts of music, Miss Raggl instructed the class to listen to the music and write down three separate words or very short phrases on one Post-it note that they associated with the music, through images evoked, memories, pictures drawn, moods – anything they wanted. She explicitly stated that there were no 'wrong' answers and that everyone's ideas were equally valid. She played an audio recording of an excerpt of the first piece – *Threnody for the Victims of Hiroshima* by Penderecki. At the end of the excerpt, she quickly pointed at each pupil in turn to say one of their words out loud, then repeated with the second and third words. There was an astonishing range of vocabulary – terror, screeching, fright, sirens, shattering – and much more.

This exercise was then repeated with two further pieces of music – *The Ashokan Farewell* by Jay Ongar (lamenting, sorrowful, thoughtful, solitude, death, lonely, Ireland, Grandad, violins were some of the words chosen) and an audio excerpt from the song *Have a Nice Day* by the Stereophonics, eliciting responses such as sunshine, happy, driving, fun and jolly. Pupils were then invited to make and share an interesting sentence built around one of their words. The teacher modelled this, reading out her own sentence: 'It started with a shrill scream of terror from Nigel, the garden gnome with the fishing rod, when he saw Monsieur Hargreaves approaching with a huge paintbrush and a can of bright red paint.'

Over the course of the week, these sentences were used as individual story openings and the Post-it notes were mounted on a board as prompts for interesting words. Using their stories as a stimulus, in the following week's music lesson, pupils were encouraged to compose music in groups to accompany one scene from the story picked by the random name generator on the whiteboard. The story and music were audio recorded and shared on the school website. This double focus developed children's understanding of the purpose and construction of programme music, alongside developing their language, creative writing and storytelling skills.

The models of cross-curricular learning explored in this chapter signify endless possibilities for musical development and learning in and through the curriculum when worthwhile and inspiring learning opportunities are seized.

Musical experiences beyond the curriculum

Music, and particularly singing, is often integral to the whole-school community, for example in assemblies, concerts, special events, being out and about in the community, extra-curricular clubs. The focus is often on participation for children of different ages and different skill levels. Extra-curricular opportunities, whether short-term or throughout the year, are a way of bringing children together who have been excited by music within the curriculum and to nurture their developing musical identities. It is important for all opportunities to be open to all children, and to share this ethos of inclusion, as there are possibly children who feel that these clubs are a closed shop. Ofsted (2009, 2012) noted that musical participation beyond the classroom is often not representative of the children in the school, for instance it is less populated by boys, travellers, those with special educational needs and disabilities, and those in receipt of free school meals. Teachers need to be really aware of the demographic of pupils in their school and to try and make musical opportunities as appealing and accessible as possible. This includes thinking about times in the school day when activities are offered because some children cannot stay after school or get to school early for a multitude of reasons. Some of the most successful and inclusive schools I have worked with create musical events with the explicit intention of including the whole school community. This is often done by developing some of the work in the classroom with each class and then further developing it in the extra-curricular groups and bringing these together to perform and enjoy making music. This takes considerable planning and effort but is a great way to develop an inclusive community ethos.

Music is unique and special. It offers possibilities for people of all skill levels, ages, physical development, with or without instruments, to work together as an effective ensemble where everyone's contribution is equally important and valued. A child playing open strings on a violin can be sat alongside a professional violinist; a child with a physical impairment can add sounds with Soundbeam into the same piece; this cannot happen on a sports pitch as the physical differences between a 5-year-old and a professional footballer create significant inequality. The skill is designing musical experiences that value and include everyone and in which everyone can contribute and celebrate being part of something amazing.

Unfortunately, some children do not thrive in an academic classroom environment and their self-determination is negatively affected by the way they feel about themselves as a learner. Teachers are instrumental in helping children to feel like successful learners. Opportunities to engage in music within and beyond the curriculum can be a lifeline for some children, helping them to find ways through the struggle of learning. Creating and highlighting opportunities for engagement inside and outside of the classroom is vitally important for all children, not just those who self-identify (and we inadvertently identify) as 'the musical ones'.

There is also much said and written about how music can help in everyday life – as a way to handle stress, to feel confident, to block something out, to change or deal with a situation or mood, to express our feelings, to connect with others – the list goes on and on. Whilst within the limited scope of this book there is insufficient room to really unpick this, we should not forget the power of music in our lives and its potential as an intervention or wellbeing tool within schools, therapy and music programmes, and as a personal choice for all of these aspects of our diverse and dynamic lives. The wellbeing of staff and children is of fundamental importance if schools are to thrive.

Routines

Music also often forms part of the routines in classrooms, particularly in early years settings. Nursery staff often sing the same songs or type of songs to accompany events such as greeting children, nappy changing, moving to the lunch table, waving goodbye to parents, etc. In many nurseries, the routine of the day is punctuated by music, even insofar as staff voices have a singsong tone; the success of this is often evident in the relationships and bonds developed between staff, individual children and groups. Some nurseries play particular recorded pieces to help young children to sleep/relax at certain times of the day, and the mood of the music creates a particular atmosphere. In some reception and infant classes, the use of music to punctuate events or routines sometimes happily continues. I have also seen music used in special educational needs settings to help children to recognise points in the day and know that there is a transition to or from a particular activity. Using music in this way is not time-consuming; it does not detract from other learning and is perhaps an untapped potential in many classrooms.

TASK 9.5

If you are a working in a pre-school, reception or infant class, think about the routines of the day. Write/draw out a rough timetable and identify where music and song already form part of this day. Then, in another colour, add in your own ideas for developing this further and try to embed them little by little over the next two weeks.

There are plentiful ways to embed music in routines with older children too. There may be a massed singsong before school on a particular day of the week, a particular piece of music played whilst children change for PE which they must try to 'beat', music played as they walk into and out of assembly, and songs sung at transition points in the day to focus attention back on the teacher. The use of music can change the mood and pace of a classroom very quickly.

Partnerships in music education

The National Plan for Music Education (DfE, 2011: 3) states: 'Great music education is a partnership between classroom teachers, specialist teachers, professional performers and a host of other organisations, including those from the arts, charity and voluntary sectors.'

Many schools are involved in partnerships with other organisations; some are of a transient, short-term nature whilst others are fully embedded in school life. One thing is for sure – schools will not be short of offers for people and organisations to deliver workshops (for a fee, and occasionally for free). There are some really excellent education departments linked to, for example, professional orchestras, national arts organisations and museums. There are also many other commercial organisations offering programmes for pupils and teachers, some of which work over a substantive period of time and are really excellent in developing a wide range of creative musical skills. Be aware of one-size-fits-all and one-off workshop offers. It is important that schools work out what would benefit their pupils rather than being drawn in by the marketing, and then seek to work with well-regarded organisations who are genuinely interested in personalising learning experiences for your pupils, not just 'delivering' an off-the-shelf offer. One-off workshops are very nice entertainment but rarely effective for learning in the longer term. Finding inspiring practitioners with the right skill set to enthuse your class and, most importantly, understand learning, is crucial if we are to go beyond music education workshops just providing entertainment without substance.

Whole-class instrumental programmes and instrumental learning

In 2001, the then Labour government gave a commitment that 'over time, every primary school child that wants to, should be able to learn a musical instrument' (DfES, 2001: 12). In order to deliver this aspiration, many children across the country have taken part in a whole-class instrumental or vocal programme lasting between a term and a year, and often delivered by a local authority music service.

Whole-class instrumental and vocal programmes – sometimes called 'First Access' or 'Wider Opportunities' – are funded by the Department of Education in England. These programmes aim to provide opportunities for all children to experience instrumental learning as a whole class for a minimum of a term and for up to a year. We need to be careful not to think of these programmes as being just about learning a musical instrument, and instead to recognise emergent learning in a broader context. John Finney's blog (2015, 2016) has some interesting entries on a programme in Cambridgeshire which is well worth a read to give you a wider context.

Over time, as the funding arrangements for this kind of music education changed, music education hubs were established. You can find out who the local hub lead in your area is by looking at the map on the ISM website. Each hub is free to decide on the model of both delivery and funding, so in some areas this programme is totally free for schools and pupils, and in other areas it is heavily subsidised but schools are expected to contribute financially. At the end of the whole-class instrumental experience, some children will hopefully want to continue to learn and play; however, at this point the access to tuition usually involves a cost either to the school or directly to the parents, and unfortunately this can be a prohibitive barrier to continuation for some children.

TASK 9.6

Find out which classes in your school are currently involved in a whole-class instrumental programme and which children have been involved in the past. Try to go and observe, or perhaps even join in with, a lesson.

Whole-class instrumental and vocal programmes can be really excellent – a downside is that children do not usually get to choose the instrument they learn, which, as McPherson et al. (2012) point out, is an important aspect of musical engagement. Despite this, where the whole-class programme is well planned and delivered by inspiring and engaging teachers in ways that develop holistic as well as instrument-specific musical skills, these programmes can contribute significantly to a child's musical education.

As a class teacher, it is all too easy to assume that the instrumental teacher leading a whole-class experience is an expert who knows what to do, what level to pitch the work at, and automatically connects the work with what your class has been doing in music lessons. This is a nice aspiration, and in the best whole-class programmes it happens, and there is communication and planning time with the class teacher. Joint planning – both before a programme of work and during it – ensures that children's prior experiences, learning needs and manifesting behaviours/attitudes are commonly understood. However, this is not always the case and you might need to work hard to help both the visiting teacher and the pupils to make it relevant and inspiring. There are some excellent instrumental teachers around, but not all have the experience as classroom teachers to work effectively with a whole class, so if you can be involved in these lessons it is often an advantage for so many reasons! Anyway, what could be more fun for you than learning a musical instrument alongside the children? It is also interesting to note that a school is responsible for the quality of any teaching which takes place there, and therefore the lessons should be appropriately differentiated and challenging and contribute to musical learning for all pupils; the school should challenge the organisation providing them if this is not the case!

Finding ways to keep the momentum going between the weekly lessons is also important. You could consider having a practice club at break time, or dedicating a short amount of time each day to practising with the class. Some children may take instruments home – indeed, for some children, being seen walking in and out of school with an identifiable musical instrument in a case is important. However, not all children will do this and it takes time and input to develop good habits that enable effective practice, and children may not get support from home either. You could also encourage the instrumental teacher to make some short video clips demonstrating what the children should be practising each week, so that they have an audio-visual model easily available through a suitable online portal such as the school website. This will also serve as a way to help parents understand what their child is involved in.

Learning a musical instrument for this limited period of time might be the only chance that a particular pupil gets for 'formal instrumental tuition', but it need not be the case if music education through your school and class offers sustainable opportunities for children to develop skills and confidence on a range of instruments. One of the biggest challenges, though, relates to how we get children who learn inside the classroom to feel that they are musicians too, since their point of reference may be others that they see having lessons outside of the classroom. Finding ways for them to continue to develop the habits, attitudes and behaviours of successful learners, and to celebrate the achievements of all children in your class, through performing together, making recordings and sharing with those beyond the classroom, can go a long way towards this.

Chapter summary

The arts are increasingly seen as a way of joining up the curriculum and making it meaningful to young people. Through the arts children express their feelings, thoughts and responses. The arts have the potential to stimulate open-ended activity which encourages discovery, exploration, experimentation and invention. (Duffy, 2006: xvi)

A constant theme throughout this book is that music is everywhere, offering great potential to permeate the rich cultural fabric of a school. Music has tremendous power to draw children into learning, to think of themselves as musical beings and to help them make sense of the world as they explore it for themselves.

Schools and teachers play a fundamental role in helping children see beyond the brow of the hill, exposing them to cultures and opportunities beyond their peripheral vision. Engaging and exciting children through enriching, inspiring, fulfilling and valuable experiences in, through and about music, opens up possibilities for current and future learning. This chapter is about placing music at the heart of the school and the curriculum. Given all of the benefits and evidence about the power of music, notwithstanding the most important – the significant impact of music learning itself – it is difficult to fathom why any school *wouldn't* aspire for music to be at the heart of the school and curriculum.

Further reading

Barnes, J. (2015) *Cross Curricular Learning 3–14*. London: Sage.

Daubney, A., Elliott, R. and Watt, F. (2014) How Folk Music, Dance and Drama Inspired Learning in Schools. Available at: www.efdss.org/images/EFDSSASSETS/EFDSS EducationDownloads/FEreview.pdf [case studies of 19 schools using folk arts across their curriculum to support learning in a range of subjects]

Daubney, A., Elliott, R. and Watt, F. (2016) How Folk Music, Dance and Drama Inspired Learning with Museums. Available at: www.efdss.org/images/EFDSSASSETS/PDFs/ Case-study-book-2016-for-Web.pdf [case studies of collaborative cross-curricular projects with schools, museums and music education hubs]

Hallam, S. (2016) Whole Class Ensemble Teaching: Final Report. Available at: http://www. musicmark.org.uk/wp-content/uploads/WCET-Final-Report.pdf [advocacy report on whole class instrumental and vocal teaching in primary schools]

Marsh, K. (2008) *The Musical Playground*. Oxford: Oxford University Press.

Resources

English Folk Dance and Song Society Resource Bank – www.efdss.org/efdss-education/ resource-bank [this award-winning online portal includes songs, planning and resources for using the folk arts as a stimulus across the curriculum]

John Finney's blog – https://jfin107.wordpress.com/2016/06/30/first-access-and-general-music-education/ [this entry on Finney's blog describes a whole-class programme in Cambridgeshire, its underlying philosophy and the importance of the habits, values and behaviours nurtured through the programme]

Minute of Listening – www.minuteoflistening.org [a subscription package which provides 60 seconds of creative listening every day for the school year; this is a fantastic resource with the potential to be extensively used to inspire learning across the curriculum]

10
BRINGING IT ALL TOGETHER

'Knowing music in the bones is what counts.' (Finney, 2015)

Introduction

As this book draws to a close, this chapter offers opportunities to review and reflect, focusing on the wholeness of music education and the place of primary music teaching as a vital stepping stone in a child's musical journey.

The potential role of music and music education in aiding the transition from primary to secondary school is considered, along with some practical ideas for improving the experiences between phases. This links directly to our need to collaborate with others if we really want to join up different parts of music education.

The book concludes where it started, in thinking about ourselves as developing music educators and reconsidering our view on music education – what it is now and what it could be.

A book such as this can only scratch the surface. Working your way through the ideas and tasks is part of a developmental journey but it is by no means the end. From here, the possibilities are endless; you are facilitated by your imagination, confidence, drive and willingness to explore new ideas and try new things.

Through this chapter you will:

- explore musical transitions between primary and secondary schools and the potential role of music
- consider how we can gather support from others and what support you might need
- reflect on your own idea about what music education is and what it is for
- review your own perspectives on yourself as a music educator and what you might do next in your own professional journey.

Onwards and upwards? Musical transition from primary to secondary school

Transition in education is a hotly debated topic, with the focus of the discussions often related to a very narrow view – an observed dip in children's academic attainment in core subjects between leaving primary school and the first few months of secondary school. Our lives are dynamic, and transitions are necessary and flexible processes that, for the most part, we manage with relative ease. However, there are certain transitional changes, particularly those involving 'rites of passage' which mark out important stages in our lives and involve key events or celebrations. Transition from one school to another – particularly leaving one phase of education and moving on to the next – is one of these. Focusing on academic attainment overlooks the potential psychological, emotional and social traumas associated with moving school – all aspects on which music can positively impact.

As with general education, research specifically situated in music education across the primary to secondary transitional phase highlights many potential areas for consideration. There is agreement on the need for children to have positive experiences *in* music education within and beyond the curriculum. Music education also has an important role in assisting with transition per se. Many of the findings of transition research thankfully look beyond academic attainment across this transition point and note the need to focus on children's social and emotional wellbeing. Galton et al.'s (1999) 'Five Bridges' model provides a well-respected holistic framework to develop transition.

It is helpful to think of parts of a child's music education as a series of islands, including:

- pre-school island
- primary school island
- Key Stage 3 island and the Key Stage 4 island (split in this way in secondary school because music ceases to be a compulsory subject in most secondary schools at some point)
- whole-class instrumental and vocal teaching island
- 'jamming with friends' island
- music at home island
- extra-curricular programme island.

These, along with many other islands, constitute the large archipelago of a child's music education. As teachers, we can have a direct impact on some of this, and part of our responsibility is to make education and experience on those islands we can influence as good as possible.

However, if each island operates in a silo, the learning and experience gained from each island may not continue to be developed on the next island. Additionally, each lone island may not benefit from the experiences brought about by children having different musical influences from a range of other islands simultaneously. Our job, therefore, involves us helping to build bridges between the islands, being flexible and dogmatic in trying to create learning experiences both on and between the islands.

In education, there is an inherent misunderstanding and perhaps intolerance about what goes on in other phases of education. I would go so far as to say that, frequently, an ignorance about music education exists between primary and secondary schools, caused, for the most part, by neither side of this 'humpback bridge' making the effort to observe and explore the learning culture of the other side. To be clear, I am not teacher bashing here; we are all extremely busy people, but unless we are able to more fully communicate with the other islands, we will remain in our silos and children's learning, experience and motivation may well suffer as a result. It seems that the problem is multi-faceted; for example, as well as teachers being busy, music is not a 'priority subject' within schools or through transition and therefore schools tend to focus their attention on core subjects. Additionally, I know that there is unfortunately a perceived hierarchy of teachers and schools and that primary teachers can feel intimidated by the idea of communicating on equal terms with secondary teachers who are almost always 'music specialists'.

In models where transition *in* and *through* music education could be deemed to be excellent, many stakeholders from multiple settings communicate well, understand each other's perspectives and are flexible around the changing needs, aspirations and experiences of all children. These stakeholders also share a vision: to provide an excellent music education for all children. They are committed to working together to achieve this, i.e. to building bridges between the islands whilst also valuing and celebrating the musical communities on each island individually and collectively. An online tracker, which is well worth engaging with, explores music across each of the following 'five bridges' identified by Galton et al. (1999):

- bureaucratic bridge
- social and emotional bridge
- curriculum bridge
- pedagogy bridge
- management of learning bridge.

Within the confines of this book, there is insufficient room to include detailed information on musical transition, and it is an on-going 'problem' that needs the sustained attention of music educators and senior leaders from a wide range of different contexts. Unquestionably, it is hard to develop relationships with other organisations and teachers, yet this is absolutely what we need to do. The following practical suggestions are extracted and adapted from a document offering advice to primary, secondary and instrumental teachers in order to assist them in joining up children's music education between the different 'islands' and also in considering the potential of music to improve other aspects of a child's experience of transition (Daubney and Mackrill, 2011). The examples chosen are from an extensive list which relates closely to the perspective of primary colleagues, yet reading around the topic more widely would certainly be beneficial (e.g. Daubney et al., 2013; Marshall and Hargreaves, 2007; Symonds et al., 2011).

Developing teachers' awareness and practice through building relationships

'Practitioner mobilisation' – where practitioners are encouraged to meet face to face to reflect on and develop their own practice by observing and working alongside colleagues in other settings and across phases – tends to be one of the most powerful agents of change in transition practices. Observing and working alongside other music teachers in linked schools enables primary and secondary teachers (and instrumental teachers/workshop leaders) to learn from each other. This idea is at the heart of joint practice development, in which a culture of enquiry is embedded through an exchange of knowledge via interactions directly related to practice (Sebba et al., 2012).

As a primary school teacher, you should not feel intimidated by observing lessons in secondary school or by having colleagues from other settings observing and working alongside you. Daubney et al.'s (2013) study noted the difficulties with setting up such a model, yet they also observed secondary school teachers' fundamental change of attitude and practices following cross-phase observations and discussions with teachers and pupils in primary schools.

We need to embed joint practice development in work if we are to get past the point of children being seen as 'empty vessels' at the start of their secondary school career. Unfortunately, some secondary teachers hold the ignorant and incorrect assumption that 'they do nothing at primary school' (Mills, 1996: 7). Greater understanding of the rich musical environments in primary school is certainly of importance if we are to move beyond the 'start from scratch' mentality that still pervades music education in some secondary schools. There can be little more that is demotivating and disheartening for a pupil than to experience a frankly dull and uninspiring music education that fails to recognise or develop their interests, strengths and passions, particularly when they were looking forward to everything that a new school has to offer and that they were shown at the open evenings.

Curriculum continuity

Practitioner mobilisation is the best way for teachers to be able to consider the appropriateness of their curriculum, pedagogies and assessment and to develop these in consideration of a wider context. Specific strategies could include talking together about the curriculum, assessment, styles of teaching and learning and focus. You may be able to identify common topics, genres and areas that could be developed in a focused way across Years 6 to 7. I have also been in situations where secondary school teachers have been shocked to observe Years 3 or 4 classes in primary school working at the same level of challenge as their own classes in Years 7 and 8.

An interesting point about curriculum relates to the focus of learning and the approaches taken in different settings. In primary school, there is often much more understanding that 'thinking and acting musically' is the way through which children develop and, in doing so, they embody knowledge and 'show' this through their actions. Sometimes the focus of learning in secondary school (unfortunately) becomes more explicitly about students being able to talk about music and show that they know what something is or what it means by verbally describing it, identifying it from a recording or writing it down in a test.

Some secondary school teachers think that primary schools should do more to make pupils 'secondary ready' – a particularly grating term that has come to mean reaching particular 'floor standards' across different (usually core) subjects. However, you need to think hard about whether your practice in primary school should change at the whim of secondary colleagues, particularly when it might go against Paynter's (1982) guiding principle that musical learning is essentially practical and experiential, and therefore making music is more important than learning information about music. The question you really have to ask yourself is whether the music education in your school and your class embodies the values you identified in Chapter 1.

Sharing children's work

Boiling a child's musical education down to a single number on a spreadsheet is totally inadequate for informing a teacher, parent or child of the rich musical experiences sitting behind it. These numbers are also greeted with scepticism and mistrust, as we all have a different impression of what a number actually means.

It is, however, beneficial to share children's musical endeavours between schools and teachers (even when transferring from one class to the next). Chapter 8 introduced the idea of sound-based digital portfolios, which could be useful if a secondary school teacher has time to engage with the work. In reality though, secondary schools have a far greater number of pupils than their feeder primaries and so work needs to be shared in practicable ways. The most effective way to do this is for a secondary school teacher to actually work together with the pupils in feeder primary schools. In reality though, pupils may come to a secondary school from a high number of feeder primary schools, particularly in metropolitan areas. However, this is not a strong enough reason not to try to develop cross-phase work and build relationships between schools, organisations and practitioners in different settings.

Another way to share work is for a primary teacher to pass on a limited number of recordings to the secondary school, along with a short note about what pupils have experienced in music through their time at primary school, and the opportunities available to them. It is also important that any pertinent short biographical details are passed on, particularly where children are learning musical instruments in school that they would like to continue in secondary school. Whilst the music education hubs may be responsible for this role, the fragmented educational landscape may mean that there is no direct continuity of teacher or provider.

'Musical passports' have been trialled numerous times but, for the most part, the amount of information is unwieldy for secondary colleagues, and these sometimes rely exclusively on the written word rather than also embedding sound. In principle, however, passports are beneficial if pupils have ownership of them and they are representative of a child's musical life both in and out of school.

Developing transition activities

There are many musical transition activities that can really benefit children as they think about moving to secondary school. Some schools and localities set up choirs or bands for children from across different year groups (e.g. Year 4 to Year 8). These are a great way for children to become familiar with their new surroundings and people, and they also provide a musical challenge beyond that offered within a school. We need to be mindful of access issues; not all parents are willing or able to get their child to a different school at the beginning or end of the day. Such opportunities do not need to be offered all year round; they could be organised just for one term a year, or even run as an intensive and immersive experience for one day per term. It is also ideal if the teacher from the primary school is a part of this band, learning and playing alongside the pupils, and offering a friendly and familiar face to pupils from their own school and to those who have already moved up. Auditioning for such groups will put many pupils off, and if they are rejected it will possibly do substantial damage to how they feel about themselves as musicians.

Other potential opportunities include inviting secondary school colleagues and ex-pupils to concerts and performances at the particular primary schools, as well as taking primary pupils to performances and joint workshops at the secondary school. Often, this is very motivating for all concerned. Some secondary schools have realised the value of bringing Year 7s back to their feeder primaries to work with the children there. We often think of transition as being a one-way process but there is significant benefit for all pupils in embedding these kinds of two-way opportunities. We should not think of transition solely taking place in the final half term of Year 6 and into the first half term of Year 7. By taking a longer-term view, we are more fully able to help children prepare for changing schools.

Some secondary schools also make music an integral part of 'transition days'. This may be a music lesson with their new class, and may also include some kind of collaborative musical performance, which often goes down well with pupils and helps to start building a community. As a teacher, you should join in with this if you are in the school too, and you may also be sent a specific piece in advance to start to work on with pupils for this occasion.

The following example reports on a specific intervention programme which used music to help children in challenging circumstances to settle into their secondary school (Daubney, 2013):

> Recognising that some pupils take longer to settle into secondary school and the potential of music to help smooth the passage, the Virtual School in Brighton and Hove, who is responsible for the education of children in care, ran an intervention programme. Over the course of the summer term, Year 6 pupils under the care of the Virtual School were invited with a friend of their choice to go on a weekly basis to their new school and have instrumental or singing lessons with specifically selected teachers from the music service. A child from Year 7, who was already known from the previous year in primary school, joined in with the small group lesson and also showed the Year 6s

around the school in the breaks. Arrangements were made through the Head of Music; the Year 6s also met the secondary pupils frequently, providing a familiar face for the new school year. New form tutors and the designated person in the school with responsibility for children in care were also invited to share work as it emerged. Children became familiar with their new surroundings and key people, and it provided a framework for them to be able to talk about their hopes and fears. Musically, they worked on something they had agreed with the instrumental tutor at the outset and produced an audio recording at the end to share with whoever they wanted. It is interesting that the children involved in the programme carried on with the small group learning in secondary school, but did not initially join in with extra-curricular musical activities due to a lack of confidence and the desire to want to make friends during break and lunch times.

TASK 10.1

Find out about transition practices taking place in your current school and think about the following.

1. Are any of these related to music education in any way?

2. Is there any curriculum continuity?

3. Are the teachers in different schools in contact with each other and do they have any experience of joint practice development in other settings?

4. Are there any ways in which music is used to support children's transition to secondary school?

Giving and receiving support

I would argue that ... most music is best taught by the class teacher – *supported by* intermittent specialist support of various kinds – in order for children to get the most exposure to, and experience of, the joy of music and singing in school. (Bremner, 2013: 79)

As a teacher, there will always be things we want to be better at, things we might want to develop and ways in which we can help others. The four questions you need to ask yourself are:

1. What do I want to do?
2. What is the best way to go about it?
3. What support do I need?
4. Who (and what) can best help and support me?

In terms of developing ourselves as music educators, there are many people in the school and wider community who can help. We need to make professional

judgements about whether the help available is actually supporting us to professionally develop and builds our confidence to lead music making in our class. As
primary school teacher Zoe Bremner (2013: 79) astutely points out in the report
on her own musical journey, entitled 'Transforming an "unmusical" primary
teacher into a confident musician', some musical opportunities offered in
schools, such as the one she describes, work against this requirement:

> Such a way of working actively distanced the teachers from the act of singing.
> They could sit on the side and be quite passive. Many teachers would further
> remove themselves from the act of singing by leaving the hall to use the half
> hour to catch up on some other school work. The way of teaching singing only
> served to lower the confidence of teachers of teaching singing, as it provided
> no opportunity to put their skills into practice. (Bremner, 2013: 86)

Zoe's report is essentially about taking responsibility for her own professional
development through the perspective of being a teacher-researcher and taking on
a critical perspective in relation to her own work, and her reflections on which
experiences were useful and which weren't. Some schools, particularly teaching
schools, are beginning to embed a culture of enquiry. It may be that this is something that you want to investigate further.

Each primary school has someone who has a designated responsibility for music,
although as Hennessy (1998: 10) points out, the language used for the person in
this role varies, as does the accompanying job description: 'curriculum leader or
music coordinator suggest that the school has clear expectations and gives similar
status to music as it does to other subjects.'

Hennessy's book, *Coordinating Music across the Primary School*, is packed full
of ideas for teachers who have responsibility for music in their place of work. It is
well worth a read for those looking for practical advice on undertaking this role and
all that it entails.

As a music teacher in a primary school, there are many offers for professional
development available, particularly those provided through local music education
hubs, their partner organisations and by providers of national programmes. The
same advice applies as with selecting external workshops for your pupils – you need
to know in advance what you want to get out of any professional development and
whether the 'training' on offer will meet those needs and stretch you professionally.
One-off workshops or training sessions are rarely impactful in changing practice.
The Teacher Development Trust (2014: 10) reports that 'professional development
opportunities that are carefully designed and have a strong focus on pupil outcomes have a significant impact on student achievement'.

All teachers have an entitlement to high-quality, subject-specific professional
development and should be supported by schools to undertake such opportunities. As with the examples of joint practice development described earlier in this
chapter, impactful professional development often results from working alongside someone within our own classroom, from observing and discussing with
other colleagues and from taking an enquiry-based approach to developing our
own practice.

TASK 10.2

Thinking about your own professional development in relation to teaching music, identify what you think you need to do next. What do you need to do to make this happen? Who can help?

It is sometimes too easy to think that we have nothing to offer others, but this is definitely not the case! We all have things we are good at, things we know we can do and those that can be potentially helpful to others. For example, you may have developed a very successful unit of work you could share; you may be very good at questioning or differentiation; you may even play the bagpipes!

TASK 10.3

Identify what you have to offer others in relation to helping them to develop their music teaching.

Going full circle

In drawing this chapter to a close, we need to return to the tasks in Chapter 1 and recognise how our thoughts on music education – and on ourselves as music educators – may have developed over time. In determining what music education is, and what we want children to get from it, we need to make sure that we don't view music education simply as a defined set of underlying skills, knowledge and understanding, but also consider the fundamental importance of the aesthetic and creative dimensions of music and music education.

TASK 10.4

Return to Task 1.5. Go back through the list of things that you identified as stumbling blocks and your personal hang-ups about teaching music and decide how you feel about them now. Discard those which are no longer relevant and decide on a plan of action to tackle those you still feel are valid and important. Then turn to the list of things that you are good at and you know that you can build on. Update this list too; it will grow as your confidence and experience develop.

Music education is what we make it. We are almightily powerful in this respect – whether or not we offer a child the magic of a music education is in our hands. But, as pointed out in Chapter 1, if we don't, how can we be sure that anyone else will? Folkestad (2006: 136) reminds us that 'a music teacher never meets a musically ignorant, untutored or uneducated pupil'. I would also argue that 'a pupil never meets a musically ignorant, untutored or uneducated teacher'. We all – teachers and pupils – have the potential to bring a huge amount to an inspiring music education and to get a huge amount from it; we need to find the confidence to believe in ourselves and to try things. At the heart of this book is the idea of a musical community; you are central to the evolving development of this.

TASK 10.5

Return to Task 1.4 and update your personal construct chart. Have your ideas about the constructs of an excellent teacher changed over time? What would you identify now? How would you self-rate yourself against these constructs? What successes are you celebrating and what personal developments have you noted? What targets will you set yourself next and how will you work on these?

Finally, we need to think not just about what a music education *is*, but what it *could be*. If we are honest, it is the case that, as teachers, we don't always observe models of what we consider to be excellent practice. Instead of continually perpetuating these models, we need to have the courage to move away, seeking and developing better models of music education in our own settings. We are in the midst of an open learning revolution. All education – especially informal learning – constantly changes as a result of the ways in which we negotiate and interact with the world. This is the case in music as it is with everything else. Problematically, the wheels of change in relation to education in school turn very slowly, if at all. Arguably, significant aspects of education in Britain are currently swimming against the tide. The introduction of 'new' grammar schools is hotly debated and school accountability measures work against principles of inclusion and take us back to an educational elitism based on our ability to pay and the lottery of the family and community we are born into.

Teachers are the foot soldiers of an educational revolution. To start a revolution, though, we need to pull other important people – children, other teachers, parents, school leadership, governors – along with us, through sharing with them the outcomes and benefits of an inspiring and valued music education. You are the person who can make a difference, who can continue to ask questions and to demand that educational change and our own work are evidence-informed (as opposed to evidence-based). Music education is on very dodgy ground in schools; if we don't all work at it now, it will be too late. A great music education opens up divergent and exciting pathways and possibilities for *all* pupils, bringing together and developing different aspects of their musical lives and encouraging in them a lifelong love of, and interest in, music. As research by Pitts (2009: 254) concludes:

Music teachers have the potential to be influential mentors who recognise and affirm the developing interests of their students, nourishing a sense of musical identity and providing opportunities for the acquisition of skills and the growth of confidence. They are remembered fondly where their own passion for music was evident, spreading enthusiasm and offering a role model for aspiring musicians. At their best, they are inspiring, nurturing and apparently tireless.

This could be you. Find the right people to help you, work at it, make it happen and enjoy the journey.

Further reading

Bremner, Z. (2013) Transforming an 'unmusical' primary teacher into a confident musician: A case of personal narrative enquiry. In J. Finney and F. Laurence (eds) *Masterclass in Music Education: Transforming Teaching and Learning*. London: Bloomsbury.

Finney, J. (2011) *Music Education in England 1950–2010: The Child-centred Progressive Tradition*. Abingdon: Ashgate.

Hennessy, S. (1998) *Coordinating Music across the Primary School*. London: Falmer Press.

Paterson, A. and Davies, L. (2005) *Rites of Passage: Effective Transition and Curriculum Continuity in Music Education*. Matlock, Derbyshire: National Association of Music Educators.

Resources

Inspire Music – http://inspire-music.org [an online portal for examples of stories of effective and inspiring practice from across music education]

Transition Tracker – www.musicmark.org.uk/members/magazine-features/transition-tracker-%E2%80%93-online-assessment-tool-and-self-evaluation-framework [an online assessment tool and self-evaluation framework]

REFERENCES

Alexander, R. (2010) Cambridge Primary Review: Key Stage 2 testing and accountability review. Available at: http://cprtrust.org.uk/wp-content/uploads/2014/11/Assessment-review-submission-FINAL.pdf

Allsup, R.E. (2015) The eclipse of a higher education or problems preparing artists in a mercantile world. *Music Education Research*, 17(3): 251–61.

Ashley, M. (2015) *Singing in the Lower Secondary School*. Oxford: Oxford University Press.

Ashworth, D. and Healey, P. (2015) GarageBand for Schools. Available at: https://itunes.apple.com/gb/book/garageband-for-schools/id969094325?mt=13

Bamberger, J. (2006) What develops in musical development? A view of development as learning. In G. MacPherson (ed.) *The Child as Musician: Musical Development from Conception to Adolescence*. Oxford: Oxford University Press.

Bance, L. (2012) Early Years Foundation Stage Framework. Sound Connections. Available at: www.sound-connections.org.uk/wp-content/uploads/2012-06-EYFS-Framework-A-musical-overview.pdf

Barnes, J. (2012) Integrity and autonomy for music in a creative and cross-curriculum. In C. Philpott and G. Spruce (eds) *Debates in Music Teaching*. Abingdon: Routledge.

Barnes, J. (2015) *Cross Curricular Learning 3–14*. London: Sage.

Barrett, S. (2006) Inventing songs, inventing worlds: The 'genesis' of creative thought and activity in young children's lives. *International Journal of Early Years Education*, 14(3): 201–20.

Beegle, A.C. (2010) A classroom study of small-group based improvisation with fifth grade children. *Journal of Research in Music Education*, 58(3): 219–39.

Bent, I.D. (2016) Musical notation. In *Encyclopaedia Britannica* [online]. Available at: www.britannica.com/art/musical-notation

Black, P. and Wiliam, D. (1998) *Inside the Black Box: Raising Standards through Classroom Assessment*. London: School of Education, King's College.

Bloom, B.S., Engelhart, M.D., Furst, E.J., Hill, W.H. and Krathwohl, D.R. (1956) *Taxonomy of Educational Objectives, Handbook 1: The cognitive domain*. New York: David McKay Co.

Bremner, Z. (2013) Transforming an 'unmusical' primary teacher into a confident musician: A case of personal narrative enquiry. In J. Finney and F. Laurence (eds) *Masterclass in Music Education: Transforming Teaching and Learning*. London: Bloomsbury.

Bruner, J. (1960) *The Process of Education*. Cambridge, MA: Harvard University Press.

Bruner, J. (1975) *Entry into Early Language: A Spiral Curriculum*. Swansea: University College of Swansea.

Butler, R. (1987) Task-involving and ego-involving properties of evaluation: Effects of different feedback conditions on motivational perceptions, interest, and performance. *Journal of Educational Psychology*, 79(4): 474–82.

Butler, R.J. and Hardy, L. (1992) The performance profile: Theory and application. *The Sport Psychologist*, 6(3): 253–64.

Campbell, P.S. (1998) *Songs in their Heads: Music and its Meaning in Children's Lives*. New York: Oxford University Press.

Campbell, P.S. (2010) Musical enculturation: Sociocultural influences and meanings of children's experiences in and through music. In M. Barrett (ed.) *A Cultural Psychology of Music Education*. Oxford: Oxford University Press.

Campbell, P.S., Connell, C. and Beegle, A. (2007) Adolescents' expressed meanings of music in and out of school. *Journal of Research in Music Education*, 55(3): 220–36.

Claxton, G. (1999) *Wise Up: Learning to Live the Learning Life*. Stafford: Network Educational Press.

Claxton, G. (2002) *Building Learning Power*. Bristol: TLO.

Clay, G., Hertrich, J., Jones, P., Mills, J. and Rose, J. (1998) *The Arts Inspected*. Oxford: Heinemann Education.

Clift, S., Manship, S. and Stephens, L. (2015) Singing for Mental Health and Wellbeing. Sidney de Hann Research Centre for Arts and Health, Canterbury Christ Church University. Available at: www.canterbury.ac.uk/health-and-wellbeing/sidney-de-haan-research-centre/documents/Singing%20for%20Mental%20Health%20report%20Dec%202015.pdf

Conroy, D.E., Willow, J.P. and Metzler, J.N. (2002) Multi-dimensional fear of failure measurement: The performance failure appraisal inventory. *Journal of Applied Sport Psychology*, 14(2): 76–90.

Craft, A. and Paige-Smith, A. (2011) What does it mean to reflect on our practice? In A. Paige-Smith and A. Craft (eds) *Developing Reflective Practice in the Early Years*. Maidenhead: Open University Press.

Daubney, A. (2007) *Evaluation Report: Phase 3 – Connecting Brighton & Hove*. Brighton and Hove Music Trust for The Arts Council.

Daubney, A. (2008) Teaching styles in music composing lessons in the lower secondary school. Unpublished PhD thesis, University of Surrey, Roehampton.

Daubney, A. (2013) Create, connect, inspire: Developing learning in and through music. Internal research report for Brighton and Hove Music and Arts/Brighton and Hove Virtual School.

Daubney, A. and Fautley, M. (2014) *The National Curriculum for Music: An Assessment and Progression Framework*. London: Incorporated Society of Musicians (ISM). Available online via www.ism.org/nationalcurriculum

Daubney, A. and Mackrill, D. (2011) Improvising Key Stage 2 to 3 Transition in Music. Available at: www.ism.org/images/files/KS2_to_3_transition_in_music.pdf

Daubney, A. and Mackrill, D. (2012) Mobile technologies in a disconnected educational world? Children's musical experiences using mobile technologies in and out of school. Presentation at ISME conference, Thessaloniki, Greece, July.

Daubney, A. and Marshall, N.J. (2011) Evaluation report: Crea8tiveSounds – Exploring barriers to participation in music for looked after children. Rhythmix for National Foundation for Youth Music, London.

Daubney, A., Elliott, R. and Watt, F. (2014) *How Folk Music, Dance and Drama Inspired Learning in Schools*. London: English Folk Dance and Song Society.

Daubney, A., Mackrill, D. and Sebba, J. (2013) *Final Evaluation Report: Musical Bridges – Transforming Transitions*. London: Paul Hamlyn Foundation.

DeNora, T. (2000) *Music in Everyday Life*. Cambridge: Cambridge University Press.

Department for Education (DfE) (2011) The Importance of Music: A national plan for music education. Available at: www.gov.uk/government/publications/the-importance-of-music-a-national-plan-for-music-education

DfE (2013) The National Curriculum for Music. Available at: www.gov.uk/government/uploads/system/uploads/attachment_data/file/239037/PRIMARY_national_curriculum_-_Music.pdf

DfE (2014a) Statutory Framework for the Early Years Foundation Stage. Available at: www.gov.uk/government/uploads/system/uploads/attachment_data/file/335504/EYFS_framework_from_1_September_2014__with_clarification_note.pdf

DfE (2014b) EYFS Profile, Principles and Processes. Available at: www.gov.uk/government/publications/early-years-foundation-stage-profile-handbook/eyfs-profile-purposes-principles-and-processes

DfE and Department for Culture, Media and Sport (DCMS) (2012) Cultural Education in England. Available at: www.gov.uk/government/uploads/system/uploads/attachment_data/file/260726/Cultural_Education_report.pdf

Department for Education and Skills (DfES) (2001) Schools achieving success. White Paper. Available at: www.educationengland.org.uk/documents/pdfs/2001-schools-achieving-success.pdf

DfES (2005) *The Music Manifesto Report Number 1*. Norwich: Crown Publications.

Duffy, B. (2006) *Supporting Creativity and Imagination in the Early Years*, 2nd edition. Buckingham: Open University Press.

Durrant, C. and Welch, G. (1995) *Making Sense of Music*. London: Cassell.

Eisner, E. (1996) Overview and evaluation of assessment: Conceptions in search of practice. In D. Boughton, E. Eisner and J. Ligtvoet (eds) *Evaluating and Assessing the Visual Arts in Education: International Perspectives*. New York: Teachers College Press.

Elliott, D. (2014) Music Education: What, Why and How? Available at: www.davidelliottmusic.com/music-matters/music-education-why-what-how/

Expert Subject Advisory Groups (ESAG) (2013) at https://sites.google.com/site/primarymusicitt

Fautley, M. (2010) *Assessment in Music Education*. Oxford: Oxford University Press.

Fautley, M. (2011) Developing musical leadership. In J. Price and J. Savage (eds) *Teaching Secondary Music*. London: Sage.

Fautley, M. and Daubney, A. (2015) *The National Curriculum for Music: A Framework for Curriculum, Pedagogy and Assessment in Key Stage 3 Music*. London: Incorporated Society of Musicians (ISM). Available at: www.ism.org/images/files/ISM_A_Framework_for_Curriculum,_Pedagogy_and_Assessment_KS3_Music_WEB.pdf

Fautley, M. and Savage, J.P. (2007) *Creativity in Secondary Education*. Tavistock: Learning Matters.

Finney, J. (2009) Cultural understanding. In J. Evans and C. Philpott (eds) *A Practical Guide to Teaching Music in the Secondary School*. Abingdon: Routledge.

Finney, J. (2015) Representing Musical Experience. Blog entry. Available at: https://jfin107.wordpress.com/2015/12/10/representing-musical-experience/

Finney, J. (2016) First Access and General Music Education. Blog entry. Available at: https://jfin107.wordpress.com/2016/06/30/first-access-and-general-music-education/

Fiske, E. (1999) Champions of Change: The impact of the arts on learning. Available at: http://artsedge.kennedy-center.org/champions/pdfs/champsreport.pdf

Fletcher Copp, E. (1916) Musical ability [online]. Available at: www.aruffo.com/eartraining/fletcher/copp.htm [Originally published in *The Journal of Heredity*, 7: 297–305.]

Folkestad, G. (2006) Formal and informal learning situations or practices vs. informal ways of learning. *British Journal of Music Education*, 23(2): 135–45.

Galton, M., Gray, J. and Rudduck, J. (1999) *The Impact of School Transitions and Transfers on Pupil Progress and Attainment*. London: DfEE.

Geoghegan, L. (2006) Why Musicianship Training According to the Principles of Zoltán Kodály. Available at: www.britishkodalyacademy.org/public_downloads/why_kodalyLG2006.pdf

Glover, J. (2000) *Children Composing 4–14*. London: RoutledgeFalmer.

Gordon, E.E. (1977) *Learning Sequence and Patterns in Music*. Chicago: G.I.A. Publications.

Hallam, S. (2015) The Power of Music. Available at: http://static1.1.sqspcdn.com/static/f/735337/25902273/1422485417967/power+of+music.pdf?token=v%2BfuOcwG2wVljLx6PeGXew7bWgU%3D

Hargreaves, D.J., Galton, M.J. and Robinson, S. (1990) The DELTA project. *Bulletin of the British Psychological Society Education Section*, 14: 47–53.

Hargreaves, D.J., Marshall, N.A. and North, A. (2003) Music education in the twenty-first century: A psychological perspective. *British Journal of Music Education*, 20(2): 147–63.

Hargreaves, E. (2013) Inquiring into children's experiences of teacher feedback: Reconceptualising assessment for learning. *Oxford Review of Education*, 39(2): 229–46.

Harlen, W. and Deakin Crick, R. (2002) A systematic review of the impact of summative assessment and tests on students' motivation for learning (EPPI-Centre Review, version 1.1). In *Research Evidence in Education Library*, Issue 1. London: EPPI-Centre, Social Science Research Unit, Institute of Education.

Henley, D. (2012) Cultural Education in England: A review of cultural education. Available at: www.gov.uk/government/uploads/system/uploads/attachment_data/file/260726/Cultural_Education_report.pdf

Henley, J. (2016) How musical are primary generalist student teachers? *Music Education Research* (online first): www.tandfonline.com/doi/full/10.1080/14613808.2016.1204278

Hennessy, S. (1998) *Coordinating Music across the Primary School*. London: Falmer Press.

Hennessy, S. (2000) Overcoming the red-feeling: The development of confidence to teach music in primary school amongst student teachers. *British Journal of Music Education*, 17(2): 183–96.

Higgins, S., Xiao, Z. and Katsipataki, M. (2012) *The Impact of Digital Technology on Learning: A Summary for the Education Endowment Foundation*. Durham: University of Durham and EEF.

Howe, M.J.A., Davidson, J.W. and Sloboda, J.A. (1998) Innate talents: Reality or myth? *Behavioural and Brain Sciences*, 21: 399–442.

Hubicki, M. and Miles, T.R. (1991) Musical notation and multisensory learning. *Child Language Teaching and Therapy*, 7(1): 61–78.

Kampylis, P. and Burki, E. (2014) Nurturing creative thinking. *International Academy of Education*. Available at: http://unesdoc.unesco.org/images/0022/002276/227680e.pdf

Kaschub, M. and Smith, J. (2009) *Minds on Music: Composition for Creative and Critical Thinking*. Lanham, MD: Rowman & Littlefield Education.

Kelly, G.A. (1955) *The Psychology of Personal Constructs*. New York: Norton.

Kemmis, S. (1985) Action research and the politics of reflection. In D. Boud, R. Keogh and D. Walker (eds) *Reflection: Turning Experience into Learning*. London: Kogan Page.

Kneyber, R. (2016) On neoliberalism and how it travels: Interview with Steven Ball. In J. Elmer and R. Kneyber (eds) *Flip the System*. Abingdon: Routledge.

Lamont, A., Hargreaves, D.J., Marshall, N.A. and Tarrant, M. (2003) Young people's music in and out of school. *British Journal of Music Edcuation*, 20(3): 229–41.

Lehmann, A., Sloboda, J.W. and Woody, R. (2007) *Psychology for Musicians: Understanding and Acquiring the Skills*. Oxford: Oxford University Press.

McCarthy, M. (2012) International perspectives. In G.E. McPherson and G.F. Welch (eds) *The Oxford Handbook of Music Education*. Oxford: Oxford University Press.

MacDonald, R. and Miell, D. (2000) Creativity in music education: The impact of social variables. *International Journal of Music Education*, 36(1): 58–68.

Macnamara, A. and Collins, D. (2009) More than the 'X' factor! A longitudinal investigation of the psychological characteristics of developing excellence in musical development. *Music Education Research*, 11: 377–92.

McPherson, G.E. and Renwick, J.M. (2001) A longitudinal study of self-regulation in children's musical practice. *Music Education Research*, 3: 169–86.

McPherson, G.E., Davidson, J.W. and Faulkner, R. (2012) *Music in our Lives*. Oxford: Oxford University Press.

Marsh, K. (2009) *The Musical Playground*. Oxford: Oxford University Press.

Marsh, K. (2010) Meaning making through musical play: Cultural psychology of the playground. In M. Barrett (ed.) *A Cultural Psychology of Music Education*. Oxford: Oxford University Press.

Marshall, N.A. and Hargreaves, D.J. (2007) Crossing the humpback bridge: Primary–secondary school transition in music education. *Music Education Research*, 9(1): 65–80.

Miller, A.H., Imrie, B.W. and Cox, K. (1998) *Student Assessment in Higher Education: A Handbook for Assessing Performance*. London: Kogan Page.

Mills, J. (1996) Starting at secondary school. *British Journal of Music Education*, 13(1): 5–14.

Mills, J. (2005) *Music in the School*. Oxford: Oxford University Press.

Mills, J. (2009) *Music in the Primary School*. Oxford: Oxford University Press.

Mills, J. and Paynter, J. (2008) *Thinking and Making: Selections from the Writings of John Paynter on Music Education*. Oxford: Oxford University Press.

Mito, H. (2004) Role of daily musical activity in acquisition of musical skill: Comparisons between young musicians and non-musicians. *Bulletin of the Council for Research in Music Education*, No. 161/162, 20th ISME Research Seminar, Las Palmas de Gran Canaria, July, 165–72.

Moore, A. (2012) *Teaching and Learning: Pedagogy, Curriculum and Culture*. London: Routledge.

Odam, G. (1995) *The Sounding Symbol: Music Education in Action*. London: Nelson Thornes.

Ofsted (2009) Making More of Music. Available at: http://webarchive.nationalarchives.gov.uk/20141124154759/; www.ofsted.gov.uk/resources/making-more-of-music-improving-quality-of-music-teaching-secondary

Ofsted (2012) Wider, Still and Wider. Available at: www.ofsted.gov.uk/resources/music-schools-wider-still-and-wider

Ofsted (2013) Music in Schools: What hubs must do. Available at: www.gov.uk/government/publications/music-in-schools-what-hubs-must-do

Our Future City (2015a) Homepage at: www.ourfuturecity.org.uk

Our Future City (2015b) Survey. Available at: http://media.wix.com/ugd/f3e230_f24cb3c9041e447b94a0c7a3c1263f8d.pdf

Paige-Smith, A. and Craft, A. (2011) *Developing Reflective Practice in the Early Years*. Maidenhead: Open University Press.

Paynter, J. (1982) *Music in the Secondary School Curriculum*. Cambridge: Cambridge University Press.

Paynter, J. and Aston, P. (1970) *Sound and Silence: Classroom Projects in Creative Music*. Cambridge: Cambridge University Press.

Philpott, C. (2016) The what, how and where of musical learning and development. In C. Cooke, K. Evans, C. Philpott and G. Spruce (eds) *Learning to Teach Music in the Secondary School*. Abingdon: Routledge.

Pitts, S. (2009) Roots and routes in adult musical participation: investigating the impact and school on lifelong musical interest and involvement. *British Journal of Music Education*, 26(3): 241-256

Pitts, S. (2012) *Chances and Choices: Exploring the Impact of Music Education*. Oxford: Oxford University Press.

Pollard, A., Black-Hawkins, K. and Cliff Hodges, G. (2014) *Reflective Teaching in Schools*. London: Bloomsbury.

Reid, L.A. (1967) The arts, knowledge and education. *British Journal of Educational Studies*, 15(2): 119–32.

Reimer, B. (1989) *A Philosophy of Music Education*. Englewood Cliffs, NJ: Prentice-Hall.

Rosenthal, R. and Jacobson, L. (1963) Teachers' expectancies: Determinants of pupils' IQ gains. *Psychological Reports*, 19: 115–18.

Ross, M., Rador, H., Mitchell, S. and Bierton, C. (1993) *Assessing Achievement in the Arts*. Buckingham: Open University Press.

Sagar, S.S., Lavallee, D. and Spray, C.M. (2009) Coping with the effects of fear of failure: A preliminary investigation of young elite athletes. *Journal of Clinical Sports Psychology*, 3: 73–98.

Sebba, J., Kent, P. and Tregenza, J. (2012) *Joint Practice Development: What Does the Evidence Suggest are Effective Approaches?* Nottingham: NCSL.

Sergeant, D.C. and Welch, G.F. (2008) Age-related changes in long-term average spectra of children's voices. *Journal of Voice*, 22(6): 658–70.

Sheridan, M.K. (1991) Increasing self-esteem and competency in children. *International Journal of Early Childhood*, 23 (1) 28-35.

Simpson, E. (1971) Educational objectives in the psychomotor domain. In M. Kapfer (ed.) *Behavioural Objectives in Curriculum Development*. Englewood Cliffs, NJ: Educational Technology Publications.

Sloboda, J. (2005) *Exploring the Musical Mind*. Oxford: Oxford University Press.

Smith, C., Dakers, J., Dow, W., Head, G., Sutherland, M. and Irwin, R. (2005) A systematic review of what pupils, aged 11–16, believe impacts on their motivation to learn in the classroom. In *Research Evidence in Education Library*. London: EPPI-Centre, Social Science Research Unit, Institute of Education, University of London.

Sounds of Intent in the Early Years (2015) Early Years Framework. Available at: http://eysoi.org

Stakelum, M. and Baker, D. (2013) The MaPS project: Mapping teacher conceptions of musical development. In M. Stakelum (ed.) *Developing the Musician: Contemporary Perspectives on Teaching and Learning*. Abingdon: Ashgate.

Stephens, J., Adams, D. Adams, K. Brewer, M. and Read, L. (1995) Teaching Music in the National Curriculum. In G. Pratt and J. Stephens [Eds.] *Teaching Music in the National Curriculum*. Oxford: Heinemann Educational Publishers.

Stilgoe, R. (no date) Sonnet on a World without Music. Available at: www.richardstilgoe.com/poems/SONNET%20ON%20A%20WORLD%20WITHOUT%20MUSIC.pdf

Street, A. (2006) The role of singing within mother–infant interactions. Unpublished PhD thesis, University of Surrey, Roehampton.

Swann, M., Peacock, A., Hart, S. and Drummond, M.J. (2012) *Creating Learning without Limits*. Maidenhead: Open University Press.

Swanwick, K. (1997) Assessing musical quality in the National Curriculum. *British Journal of Music Education*, 14(3): 205–15.

Swanwick, K. (1999) *Teaching Music Musically*. London: Routledge.

Swanwick, K. and Tillman, J. (1986) The sequence of musical development: A study of children's composition. *British Journal of Music Education*, 3: 305–9.

Symonds, J., Long, M., Hargreaves, J. and Chappell, A. (2011) *Changing Key: Adolescents' Views on how School Transition Shapes their Musical Development – Final Report*. London: Paul Hamlyn Foundation. Available at: www.researchgate.net/publication/272475648

Teacher Development Trust (2014) Developing Great Teaching: Lessons from the international reviews into effective professional development. Available at: http://tdtrust.org/wp-content/uploads/2015/10/DGT-Summary.pdf

Thomas, R.B. (1970) *MMCP Synthesis: A Structure for Music Education*. Bardonia, NY: Media Materials.

Turner, M. (2008) Developing Children's Musical Ability and Musical Independence through Scaffolding. Arts in Context Education Series. Available at: www.smallstepsmusicllc.com/uploads/2/5/0/4/25046540/developing_childrens_musical_ability_and_musical_independence_through_scaffolding.pdf

Urdan, T. and Turner, J.C. (2007) Competence motivation in the classroom. In A.J. Elliot and C.S. Dweck (eds) *Handbook of Competence and Motivation*. New York: The Guilford Press.

Vohs, K.D. and Baumeister, R.F. (2004) *Handbook of Self-regulation: Research, Theory and Applications*. New York: The Guildford Press.

Walker, R. (1996) In search of a child's musical imagination. In G. Spruce (ed.) *Teaching Music*. London: Routledge.

Wanlin, C.M., Hrycaiko, D.W., Martin, G.L. and Mahon, M. (1997) The effects of a goal setting package on the performance of speed skaters. *Journal of Applied Sport Psychology*, 9: 212–28.

Welch, G., Himonides, E., Saunders, J., Papageorgi, I., Vraka, M., Preti, C. and Stephens, C. (2009) *Researching the Second Year of the National Singing Programme in England: An Ongoing Impact Evaluation of Children's Singing Behaviour and Identity*. London: Institute of Education.

Wiliam, D. (2009) Assessment for learning: Why, what and how? An inaugural professorial lecture by Dylan Wiliam. London: Institute of Education, University of London.

Wood, D. (1998) *How Children Think and Learn*, 2nd edition. Oxford: Blackwell Publishing.

Wooten, V. (2013) Music as a Language. TED talk, 29 May. Available at: www.youtube.com/watch?v=2zvjW9arAZ0

Wright, R. (2012) Policy and practice in music education. In C. Philpott and G. Spruce (eds) *Debates in Music Teaching*. Abingdon: Routledge.

Young, S. (2007) Digital technologies and music education. In K. Smithrim and R. Upitis (eds) *Listen to their Voices*. Waterloo, Canada: Canadian Music Educators' Association.

INDEX